For the Greater Glory of God

A Spiritual Retreat with St. Ignatius

Manuel Ruiz Jurado, S.J.

Translated by Robert E. Hurd, S.J.

The Word Among Us Press
9639 Doctor Perry Road
Ijamsville, Maryland 21754
www.wordamongus.org

ISBN: 0-932085-78-4

Adapted and translated from the Spanish *Por El, Con El y en El . . . Toda Gloria*, © 1990 by Colección TAU, Avila, Spain, and from the Italian *Per Cristo, Con Cristo, e in Cristo*, © 1996 by Segretariato Nazionale dell'Apostolato della Preghiera, Rome, Italy, by Robert E. Hurd, S.J.

Cover design by David Crosson

Made and printed in the United States of America.

Library of Congress Cataloging-in-Publication Data

Ruiz Jurado, Manuel, 1930-
[Por El, con el y en el, toda gloria. English]
For the greater glory of God : a spiritual retreat with St. Ignatius / Manuel Ruiz Jurado ; translated by Robert E. Hurd.
p. cm.
Includes bibliographical references.
ISBN 0-932085-78-4 (pbk.)
1. Ignatius, of Loyola, Saint, 1491-1556. Exercitia spiritualia. 2. Spiritual exercises. I. Ignatius, of Loyola, Saint, 1491-1556. II. Title.

BX2179.L8 R8513 2002
248.3—dc21

2002071453

Through him,
with him,
in him,
in the unity of the Holy Spirit,
all glory and honor is yours,
almighty Father,
for ever and ever.
Amen.

—Eucharistic Prayer, concluding doxology

Contents

Welcome to the Spiritual Exercises / 8

Meet St. Ignatius / 10

Getting Started

As You Begin / 14

The Principle and Foundation / 19

The Daily Review / 27

Through Him

Step One: Purification / 30

First Exercise: A Meditation on Sin / 32

Second Exercise: Contrition / 37

Third Exercise: Conversion / 42

About Your Daily Review / 48

The Spiritual Battle: Discernment of Spirits / 53

Fourth Exercise: A Meditation on Death / 61

Fifth Exercise: A Meditation on Hell / 67

Penance and the Eucharist / 72

With Him

Step Two: The Call and the Response / 74

A Meditation on the Call / 76

How to Contemplate the Life of Christ / 83

Contemplation of the Incarnation / 86

More on Contemplating the Life of Christ / 91

The Birth of Jesus / 92

For a Better and More Perfect Discernment / 97

Mysteries of the Life of Christ / 99

The Presentation of Jesus in the Temple and the Purification of Our Lady / 99

The Flight into Egypt and the Return / 101

Jesus Remains in the Temple Without His Parents' Knowledge / 103

The Hidden Life of Nazareth / 106

Preparation for the "Elections" / 109

A Meditation on the Two Standards / 109

Three Classes of Persons / 117

Three Ways of Being Humble / 121

The Elections / 126

An Outline of Review Points for Reforming My Life / 129

Other Mysteries of the Life of Christ / 132

The Baptism of Jesus / 132

The Call of the Apostles / 135

The Banquet in the House of Simon the Pharisee / 137

Christ on the Waves / 140

The Resurrection of Lazarus / 142

In Him

Step Three: The Fullness of the Paschal Mystery / 146

Meditating on Christ's Passion and Death / 148

The Last Supper / 149

The Agony in the Garden / 152

Jesus Is Arrested and Condemned / 155

Jesus Is Sentenced to Death / 157

Jesus Is Scourged and Crowned with Thorns / 159

They Led Him Away to Crucify Him / 161

Identifying with Christ in His Suffering / 164

Christ's Sufferings and Humiliations / 164

The Passion in the Senses of Christ / 166

Meditating on the Resurrection / 168

The Resurrection of Christ and His Appearance to Our Lady / 169

The Appearance to the Disciples on the Road to Emmaus / 173

The Appearance at the Lake / 175

The Mission Transmitted / 178

The Ascension of Christ Our Lord / 180

Contemplation to Attain Love / 184

The True Meaning of the Church / 190

Welcome to the Spiritual Exercises!

You are about to begin a special journey toward God—one that many people have made before you and that is more popular today than ever. It is an exciting journey of spiritual discovery and interior transformation. Guided by the insights of St. Ignatius of Loyola, you can move into a joyful way of living and decision making that will bring greater glory to God and help you to realize the purposes for which he made you.

I know from personal experience how beneficial the *Spiritual Exercises* can be. I have guided many people through them over the years, both in individual meetings and retreats and through the Spanish, Portuguese, Italian, and Korean editions of this book. St. Ignatius speaks to a wide variety of people: lay women and men, priests, religious, young and old, spiritual beginners and the more mature. The fruit I have already seen is what now encourages me to offer this English-language guide to the *Exercises*. I hope that it will be a useful tool for anyone who wishes to draw nearer to God or to help others do the same.

In this book, I have not presented the entire *Spiritual Exercises*. Rather, I have selected the most important sections (actual words of St. Ignatius are in italics) and added my commentary and some questions for reflection. This is as St. Ignatius intended. He offered the *Exercises* as a flexible guide that spiritual directors and others could adapt according to different situations. Also, St. Ignatius was primarily concerned that the *Exercises* be put into practice—a goal that the workbook format of this guide is meant to encourage. As the late Jesuit scholar George Ganss has observed, Ignatius' work "is comparable to a book on 'how to play tennis'; almost all the intended benefit accrues to one who not merely reads it, but carries out the practices suggested."

The theme of this guide, taken from the Eucharistic Prayer, points to the goals of the *Exercises* and to the way I have divided up the selections from the four "weeks" of material proposed by St. Ignatius. "Through Him" recalls Christ and the Redemption, which frees us from sin—themes treated in the first week of the original *Exercises*. "With Him" alludes to Christ's call to join him in building the kingdom—themes from the second week. "In Him" is about embracing the paschal mystery into which Christ has incorporated us—themes that Ignatius addressed in weeks three and four.

For your journey through the *Spiritual Exercises*, be sure to take along the most important provisions: goodwill, a thirst for God, generosity, and perseverance. Offer yourself to the Lord in humility; he will know how best to fill you with his gifts. And rest assured that no matter how great your own desire for holiness and intimacy with God may be, God's desire to give you this gift is infinitely greater.

May your journey "through him, with him, in him," bring "all glory and honor" to our almighty Father! And may the most holy Virgin help and guide us by her intercession and her marvelous example of total openness to the will of God.

Manuel Ruiz Jurado, S.J.
Rome, Feast of the Annunciation of the Lord 2002

St. Ignatius of Loyola (1491-1556) was not the likeliest candidate for a career in church renewal and spiritual direction. Born into the Basque nobility, he wasted his early adult life on "the follies of the world," as he wrote in his *Autobiography*, and had a special liking for "warlike sport, with a great and foolish desire to gain fame." His quest for military glory ended abruptly in 1521, when a cannonball hit him in the legs.

Bedridden and bored while convalescing at the family castle in Loyola, Spain, Ignatius asked to read novels of chivalry; instead he was handed a life of Christ and a collection of lives of the saints. Almost despite himself, he became "rather fond" of what he found written there and began keeping spiritual notes as an aid to meditation and memory. Before long, Ignatius was asking himself, "What if *I* should do what St. Francis did, and what St. Dominic did?"

Ignatius made his choice for Christ. In 1522, when he was back on his feet, he made a pilgrimage to the shrine of Our Lady of Montserrat. He hung his sword on the altar and spent the next year in nearby Manresa—praying, doing penances and works of mercy, and helping others to find God. Writing of himself in the third person, Ignatius later observed that during that time, he liked "to note some things in his copybook; this he carried around very faithfully, and he was greatly consoled by it." These notes were the seeds of the *Spiritual Exercises*.

After a yearlong Holy Land pilgrimage, Ignatius spent nearly a decade in study so that he could prepare himself for more effective service to the Church. While at the University of Paris, he led students and even professors through the *Exercises* and he began to train others to do the same. Ignatius' zeal and spirituality, combined with his warm and winning personality, had their effect. In 1534, Ignatius and six friends vowed to follow Christ together by preaching in the Holy Land or, alternatively, by putting themselves at the service of the pope. Their decision laid the groundwork for the Society of Jesus, which was constituted as a new religious order in 1540, three years after Ignatius' ordination to the priesthood.

Ignatius spent the rest of his life in Rome, governing his fast-growing order and overseeing developing apostolates such as foreign missions and education. He continued to promote the *Exercises* and also provided spiritual and apostolic direction through a voluminous correspondence. He made time to found institutions for the education of converts, at-risk girls, orphans, and prostitutes. None of this activity came at the expense of prayer. A personal spiritual diary that Ignatius kept during the 1540s attests that his interior life grew ever deeper and more closely united to Christ. As one of his friends remarked, Ignatius was "a contemplative person even while he was in action," searching in everything for the greater glory of God.

Today, through his *Spiritual Exercises*, St. Ignatius helps us to pursue that same ideal of *praying* and *doing*.

Suggestions for further reading:

Ignatius of Loyola: The Spiritual Exercises *and Selected Works*, ed. George E. Ganss, S.J. *The Classics of Western Spirituality*. New Jersey: Paulist Press, 1991.

David L. Fleming, S.J. *Draw Me Into Your Friendship: The Spiritual Exercises. A Literal Translation & a Contemporary Reading*. St. Louis: The Institute of Jesuit Sources, 1996.

John W. O'Malley, S.J. *The First Jesuits*. Cambridge, Mass: Harvard University Press, 1995 [Paperback edition].

Joseph Tetlow, S.J. *Choosing Christ in the World. Directing the Spiritual Exercises of St. Ignatius Loyola According to Annotations Eighteen and Nineteen*. St. Louis: Institute of Jesuit Sources, 1989.

Getting

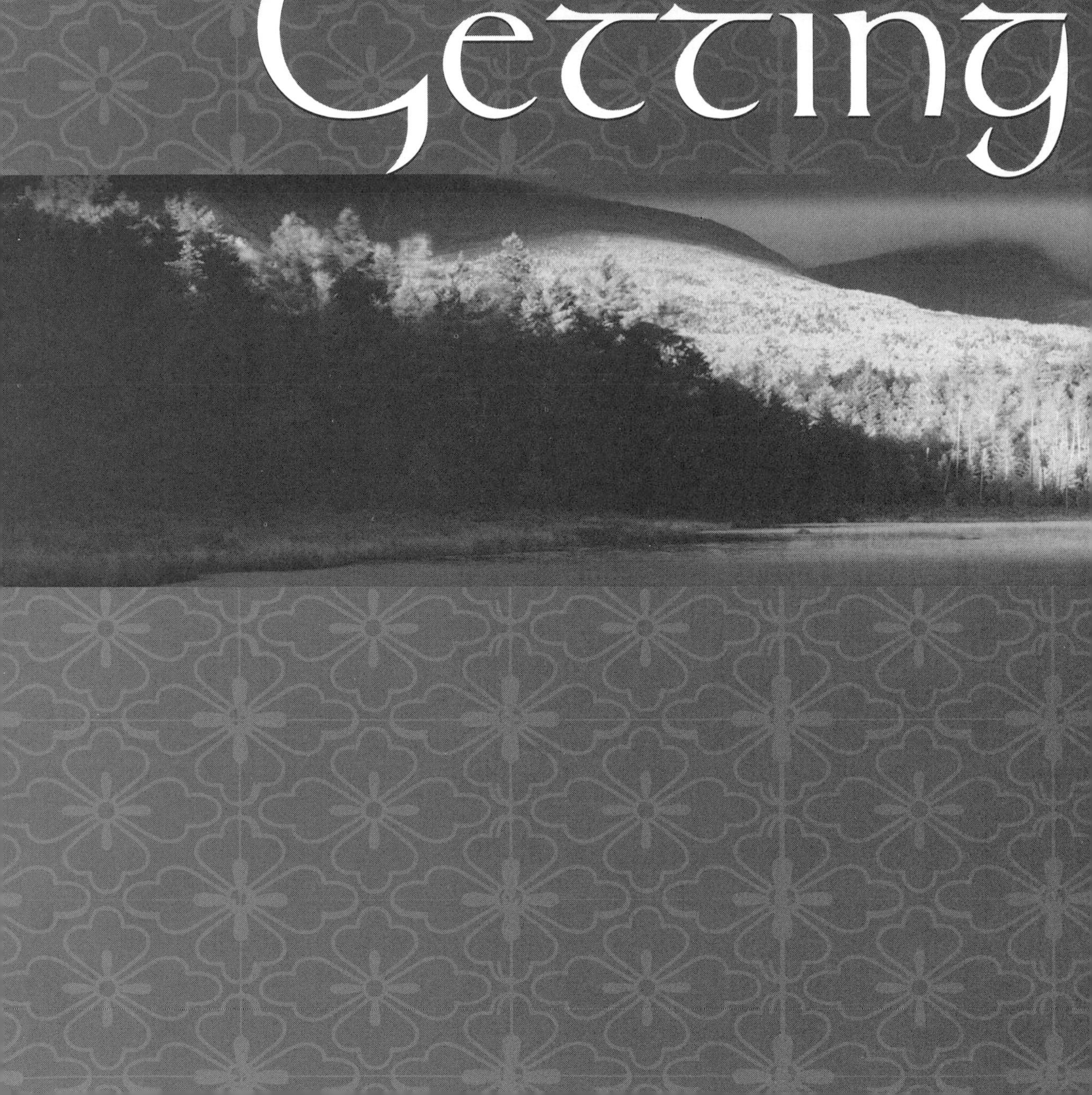

Started

You will obtain the most benefit from your journey through the *Spiritual Exercises* if you have some idea of where you are going and how you are getting there. Here are a few basics to orient you.

What are "spiritual exercises"?

Say "exercise" and most of us think about jogging, swimming, walking, or some other form of physical activity. Here, although the goal is spiritual rather than physical well-being, a comparison with physical exercise can be useful.

A good training plan uses a combination of aerobics, weight training, and other exercises to strengthen various parts of the body. Individual exercises are chosen and modified according to the desired goal. Similarly, the *Spiritual Exercises* aim at spiritual health through the use of various combined forms of spiritual activity—"exercises" such as self-examination, meditation, and other forms of prayer. The goal is *to overcome oneself, and to order one's life* in accord with the will of God (*Spiritual Exercises*, 21*). For St. Ignatius, the indicator of spiritual health is whether it is the divine will and not disordered desires and emotions that guides a person's decision making.

The goal set by St. Ignatius is not easy to achieve. Fortunately, it is not essentially a question of unaided human effort and determination, but a work of grace. Even so, learning to cooperate with grace requires instruction and practice to open ourselves to the gifts of God. We will find that prayer and self-denial are especially important "exercises" for helping us to rid ourselves of all that impedes our ability to seek and find God's will for us and to order our lives accordingly.

How much time do the Spiritual Exercises require?

St. Ignatius envisioned a period of about four weeks for the full set of *Spiritual Exercises*. He proposed four or five exercises a day, each one comprising about an hour of prayer. It did not occur to him to adapt this into an eight- or ten-day program, although this is the more common practice today. People either went through all the exercises or just some of them, according to their dispositions and abilities (*Spiritual Exercises*, 18). In both cases, the method was to

---

* Numbers refer to specific sections of the *Exercises* and are standard in every edition,

ponder one meditation after another, keeping in mind the goal of the entire process: to overcome self-will in order to live according to the will of God.

At the same time, St. Ignatius recognized that many people are not in a position to give the *Exercises* their undivided attention for an entire month. He asked these persons to consider dedicating several hours a day to the *Exercises*, over a more extended period. Using the same basic approach, they could advance step by step through the same phases of this personal adventure, making necessary adaptations and approaching the rest of their day in the spirit of the *Exercises*, as much as possible.

However, since the *Exercises* are a flexible tool, other adaptations are possible. This guidebook will help you to move through them according to the approach and dynamic that St. Ignatius intended, but at your own pace.

Can the Spiritual Exercises be done at home, or is it necessary to go away on retreat?

As much as possible, the *Exercises* should be made in a "desert" environment—a place of solitude where we are obliged to confront the presence of God face-to-face within the depths of our own consciousness. This solitude is often harsh and difficult. We naturally tend toward escape from ourselves and from God's demands. For this reason, we achieve solitude most easily when we can uproot ourselves from our places of daily activity, where we might easily slide into distractions and superficiality.

But again, adaptation is possible. At least we can achieve some solitude during the hours assigned to the exercises themselves. The essential requirement is that we strive to close the door to self-evasion. We must enter into the *Exercises* with determination to face the struggle. The "desert" forces us to admit our own weakness and look to God as our only strength. It helps us to realize that we cannot become completely closed within ourselves. In the moment of crisis that accompanies the desert experience, we hear God's saving call resonating in the silence of our nothingness, pushing us to transcend ourselves. This is an experience of dying with Christ—a necessary prelude to the resurrection.

If you do the *Exercises* at home, then, try to find ways to cultivate this desert spirit of solitude and attention to God. Can you make adjustments in your work schedule or cut back on activities and social contacts? What about setting aside a regular time for prayer—and in a quiet place where you won't be interrupted? Can you attend Mass on a daily basis, as St. Ignatius suggests (*Spiritual Exercises*, 20), or participate in the intercessory prayer of the Church through the Liturgy of the Hours?

Whichever road you choose, set out on it with vigor and generosity. Let God lead you into the desert and look to him with trust that he will "speak tenderly" to you there (Hosea 2:14). Listen attentively, and in your inner self you will hear the word of God directed to your heart.

What about a spiritual director?

The *Spiritual Exercises* began as a set of notes that St. Ignatius wrote to train people he knew in giving the *Exercises*. Then, starting in 1548 when the book appeared in print, other directors began to use it too. It is my hope that *For the Greater Glory of God* will also be a help to spiritual directors and ordinary Catholics alike.

This workbook may be used on its own. If possible, however, go through the *Exercises* with a knowledgeable guide, or speak with one periodically. It is an invaluable help to consult someone who has already traveled the road of prayer and interior struggle and knows its difficulties from experience. Also, a spiritual director who discusses your experience of the *Exercises* with you as you go along will know how to adapt them for your maximum benefit. Finally, having a good director will ensure that you go through the *Exercises* guided by the Church's teaching and authority.

If you do not have a spiritual director, perhaps there is some other person with knowledge of Ignatian spirituality whom you could ask to help you through the *Exercises*. If not, you can still benefit greatly from following them on your own, assisted by this workbook.

What are some of the benefits of the Spiritual Exercises?

The answer varies according to God's work within each individual, but in general, anyone who approaches the *Exercises* sincerely and wholeheartedly will gain greater clarity about how to discern their place in God's larger plan and how to live accordingly. People often come to the *Exercises* for help in making major life decisions, but the experience is valuable for decision making at any stage of life.

St. Ignatius offered approaches to prayer and Scripture that can inspire and equip you to persevere on the path of holiness.

How should I use this book?

- Decide how much time you can give to the *Spiritual Exercises* overall. An hour a day for a month or for a liturgical season, such as Lent? Eight or ten full days? A monthlong retreat? Whatever you choose, be realistic!

- Set aside a regular time and place for your journey with St. Ignatius. Move through the exercises in this workbook at your own pace, without rushing. Give yourself time to think about the reflection questions and then to write down something about your thoughts, inspirations, interior motions, or insights.

- Ask the Holy Spirit to lead and inspire your times of prayer.

- This workbook features a selection of excerpts from the *Spiritual Exercises*. Throughout, Ignatius' own words appear in italics. Consider obtaining a copy of the *Exercises* to supplement these excerpts. The translation I have used is *The Spiritual Exercises of Saint Ignatius*, by George E. Ganss, S.J. (Institute of Jesuit Resources, 3601 Lindell Blvd., St. Louis, MO 63108/ (314) 977-7257).

- Remember that St. Ignatius devised the *Exercises* to be flexible, and use this workbook accordingly. The material it presents is sufficient for an eight- or ten- or thirty-day retreat. You can break it up into sections, depending on your time and pace. If you wish, you can expand it by adding exercises such as the "three methods of praying" (*Spiritual Exercises*, 238-260), applying them to subjects like the commandments, the capital sins, the imitation of Christ or Mary, and Psalm 51. Also, see St. Ignatius' suggestions about how to supplement the meditations on Christ's life (*Spiritual Exercises*, 261-312).

- Keep in mind that your journey through the *Spiritual Exercises* can be taken more than once. Many people who have been able to make the all-day, monthlong Ignatian retreat find renewed spiritual benefit in making a yearly retreat of eight or ten days. Those who begin with a shorter retreat or by doing them at home are often motivated to seek a longer and fuller experience with the *Exercises* at some future point in time.

  Also, take note of specific exercises that inspired you the first time around. Revisiting them in the future will not only deepen your understanding, but will also rekindle your love, zeal, and desire for God.

- Ask the Lord to help you enter into the experience of the *Exercises* with courage, generosity, and enormous confidence in him. The stakes are high, but you will not lack his help if you place your trust in him. Remain open, and don't shrink from anything that comes from him. Take a tip from the lowly sponge, which absorbs water not when it is squeezed, but when its pores are expanded. Let your spirit expand too, and fling yourself into the immense sea of the Spirit!

Words of St. Ignatius *

What is life all about? What is *my* life all about? St. Ignatius addresses this question with a clear statement that emphasizes the basic purpose of every human life: *Human beings are created to praise, reverence, and serve God our Lord, and by means of doing this to save their souls.* Nothing is more important than recognizing and realizing this goal! In fact, *the other things on the face of the earth are created for the human beings, to help them in the pursuit of the end for which they are created.*

Our guideline, then, should be *to use these things to the extent that they help us toward our end, and free ourselves from them to the extent that they hinder us from it.* This calls for a detachment from created things—"indifference," Ignatius calls it.

We ought not to seek health rather than sickness, wealth rather than poverty, honor rather than dishonor, a long life rather than a short one, and so on in all other matters. Rather, we ought to desire and choose only that which is more conducive to the end for which we are created.

(Spiritual Exercises, 23)

* "Words of St. Ignatius" sections present direct quotes from St. Ignatius in italics. Summaries and paraphrases are in regular type.

For Reflection

Are you convinced that God loves you and has a wonderful plan for your life?
Why or why not?

What are you living for?

How would you describe your approach to things like food, clothing, computers, movies, cars? In general, do they function as helps or as hindrances to your spiritual life?

When have you had to make hard choices in order to follow the Lord?

Commentary

You Alone Are the Lord. Alone in the presence of our Creator, we feel the need to talk over our situation. How obvious our personal limitations appear to us! How great our desires! Is the Lord really listening and encouraging us in the journey we are about to begin? We need assurance that he is.

We are not solitary beings condemned to a meaningless existence. Deep within us, we hear a radiant voice saying, "*Ego sum*—I AM" (Exodus 3:14). It is the voice of the One who is, the One who loves and sustains all that exists. Before this God, I come and kneel as his creature. Lord, how much I desire to discover the loving plan for which you brought me into existence!

There is only one way to put my life in order and give it its true meaning: to acknowledge my Creator and be attentive to his design in creating me. God is the one absolute reference point for my life. I must therefore dedicate myself first of all to becoming newly aware of his active inner presence, which is intimate, fatherly, all-knowing, holy, and sanctifying. God has a plan for me and desires to bring it to completion as I freely respond to his loving invitation.

In my prayer I will ask that God truly be the Lord of my life, as he deserves to be. "*Tu solus Dominus*. You alone are Lord" (Deuteronomy 6:4-7)! May I recognize the touch of his creating, sanctifying hand. God chose me "before the foundation of the world," that I might be "holy and blameless before him" and destined in love for "the praise of his glorious grace" in his beloved Son (Ephesians 1:4-6).

Whatever this love requires of me, may it all be renewed! Recognizing God's fatherly love and praising him with joy, I offer:

- my awareness, in reverent adoration, of God's infinite *majesty and holiness*,
- my acknowledgment, in joyful praise, of his infinite *goodness and nobility*,
- my acceptance—demonstrated not just in my words but in my total self-giving to the service of his will—of his *unique Lordship*,
- my recognition that only by following God's plan will I see myself freed from all forms of slavery and arrive one day to the eternal life of unending Love for which I was created.

God is the only Absolute. Before him, everything else becomes relative. I will ask the Lord to help me really grasp this. I will also ask for the grace to know and understand that all created things are fleeting, conditional, and intended to serve God's purposes. We human beings were not made for things. Rather, they were made for us, and we were made for God in Christ.

God is the only God. Ask yourself whether your life reflects this truth, or whether you are allowing yourself to serve false gods: possessions, reputation, personalities, inclinations, your own or others' plans. Everything, even the needs of others, must yield before God's loving plan for you, which is part of his universal plan to save all creation in Christ through his Church.

The challenge is to recognize that created things attain their true value only to the extent that they lead to the fulfillment of God's plan. For this reason, we must accept or make use of them when they are useful for accomplishing God's will, but forego or flee them when they are not. As we follow this norm, we will contribute to a world in which everyone and everything work together for the praise of God's glory.

For Reflection

Jesus said that "no one can serve two masters" (Matthew 6:24). Whose servant are you? Or, to use another image, who or what is in the driver's seat of your life?

What's wrong with pursuing relationships, causes, and things without considering what purposes God intends them to serve? How can pursuing things that may be good in themselves sometimes lead to confusion and sin? Can you think of examples?

Think about the fact that God is with you and truly present as you turn to him. Speak to him from the heart—about your desire to know him better . . . to discover and cooperate with his plan for you and for the world . . . to put him above everything else in your life.

Your Will, Lord, Not Mine. God alone is Lord, and his is the only plan that saves. Once I see this and yearn to adopt his plan as the sole norm of my existence, then how can I possibly make life decisions based on anything else? Certainly I must not allow myself to be ruled by my attraction or distaste for certain people or things or by my preference for abundance over scarcity, pleasure over pain, applause over ridicule. In all my decision making, the Lord's will must be my only guide. Otherwise, how quickly my natural likes and dislikes will become my true motives! Unless I am on guard, they will lead me to go against God's plan and get sidetracked from the goal of my existence.

The will of God should orient all my relationships so that I can always say, "I want only what you want, Lord." And whenever I experience contrary tendencies or desires, I must say, like Jesus, "Not my will, but yours, be done, Lord. Not as I will, but as you will" (Luke 22:42; Matthew 26:39).

This does not mean ignoring the sentiments of the human heart. Rather, the goal is to give them their proper orientation: to desire what God desires, and in the way he desires it; to detest what he detests, to the extent that he detests it. This means not second-guessing God's will or insisting on my own preferences. For example, if it pleases God that I be ignored or that I come to him sooner rather than later, I must not seek esteem or long life. I must respond this way in everything:

- even if God asks me to surrender something he has promised me, as he asked Abraham to surrender Isaac, the child of the promise (Genesis 22);

- even if he asks me to leave everything and follow him, as Jesus did the rich young man (Matthew 19:16-29);

- even if he tells me to let the dead bury their dead (Luke 9:59-60).

Looking at our own concrete situations, we see more clearly how much we still need to bring order into our emotional life. What a struggle it is to arrive at the state of mind which always desires and chooses whatever best serves God's plan for us—and through us, for all creation! My entire being must be put into harmony in order to overcome these areas of resistance. Inevitably, I must die in Christ to all that is disordered in me so that I may rise renewed and in harmony with him. Then I will be entirely at the service of God's plan, fully disposed to choose what will best serve the purpose for which God has created me.

Those who exercise this self-mastery have attained to what St. Ignatius calls *indifference*. Indifference is the emotional distance that permits us to look at things objectively in order to make decisions in the spirit of Christian liberty (1 Corinthians 7:29-31).

Most of us have yet to arrive at this truly Christian disposition of mind and heart. When we say things like "let's not even discuss that" or "that's too hard" or "oh, that's not important," aren't we revealing our lack of indifference? Don't such remarks indicate that we harbor certain predetermined decisions because we lack this indifference?

We should always be honest and realistic in admitting the wayward inclinations and resistance that result because we lack this indifference. We should resolve to free our wills from prejudice and partiality so that we confront our set ideas and learn to make decisions in accord with God's will and not our own.

In this, we have great cause for hope. It is true that the love of things has often made us indifferent to God. But how much more can our love of God make us indifferent to the attractions and repulsions we feel toward created things! How we need this absolute, single-minded love! Before it, everything else is worth nothing.

Pray insistently, then, for an absolute, loving reverence for our infinitely majestic Lord. Let yourself be totally overcome by his saving love. Spontaneously, your reverence will give rise to the desire to purify and unite yourself more and more to God in perfect fulfillment of his will. Always want and choose what leads to him most completely. Keep yourself ready to sacrifice even your most cherished desires.

Read Psalm 139. Linger wherever you experience a greater sense of devotion, wherever you sense the Lord communicating himself to you.

Ask the Lord to help you assimilate the two steps emphasized in this "principle and foundation" section:

- God's lordship and love
- your unselfish response.

The Daily Review

St. Ignatius saw the end-of-day examination of conscience, or examen, as an important way to grow closer to God. Use the following questions and guidelines to help you stay on track as you go through the *Spiritual Exercises*.

- *Have I been faithful to prayer today?*
  Show your generosity to God by not allowing anything to curtail the time you decided to set aside for these exercises. Remember that you are being led to prayer by the Holy Spirit.

- *Has my fidelity to prayer been only external, or has it been a real search for God and an exercise of my faith?*
  It is important to open yourself to God's word so that you can assimilate it and let yourself be enlightened by its true meaning, as transmitted by the Church. In this way, your being will be transformed according to God's plan for you.

- *Have I allowed the Lord to challenge me down to the deepest corners of my being?*
  Let yourself feel the sting as he cleanses your open wounds with his merciful hands.

- *Have I arrived at a relaxed silence and atmosphere of solitude, where I can be serenely open to the divine communications which the Lord intends?*
  Tension and nervousness are worrisome signs. If you experience them, try to identify the causes and bring them to Christ. A good spiritual director can help you with this.

- *Did I prepare well for today's exercises?*
  Don't neglect anything that might help you become more attentive to the points for meditation: taking notes, rereading the material, looking up the Scripture texts or spending more time with them.

- *During today's exercises, did I maintain an attention which was alert without being anxious?*
  Consider the material peacefully—without haste or concern to move on and finish everything in a hurry, but allowing yourself to pause wherever you find light, grace, or an impulse of love. Remember that our spirits are not satisfied by much learning but by feeling and savoring things in their inner being.

- *Have I realized that as I go through the exercises, each day prepares the next?*
  How you approach today's subjects for meditation and cultivate a "retreat" environment will affect tomorrow's prayer. The thoughts, images, and feelings you have as you go to bed tonight will affect your waking tomorrow. For this reason, you will find it helpful to end each day by looking over the next day's subjects for meditation.

- *Have I kept my goal in pursuing these exercises firmly before me?*
  As a help, St. Ignatius advises that we begin every time of meditation with a *preparatory prayer* to *ask God our Lord for the grace that all my intentions, actions, and operations may be ordered purely to the service and praise of the Divine Majesty* (*Spiritual Exercises*, 46).

- *Have I taken note of the inspirations and movements of grace that I experienced today?*
  It is important not to overlook these in your daily review. Noticing and even writing down those instances where you felt God's comforting and strengthening presence is one way to arrive at understanding God's will for your life.

Through

Step One

purification

A Meditation on Sin

Words of St. Ignatius

St. Ignatius proposes three "points" for reflection—here, three instances of sin—as a help to stirring up that hatred for sin which is needed to reject it. The overall prayer petition of this exercise is *to ask for shame and confusion about myself, when I see how many people have been damned for committing a single mortal sin, and how many times I have deserved eternal damnation for my many sins. . . .*

Point One: I will call to memory the sin of the angels: How they were created in grace and then, not wanting to better themselves by using their freedom to reverence and obey their Creator and Lord, they fell into pride, were changed from grace to malice, and were hurled from heaven into hell. Next I will use my intellect to ruminate about this in greater detail, and then move myself to deeper emotions by means of my will.

Point Two: Consider the sin of Adam and Eve. *I will call to memory . . . how Adam was created in the plain of Damascus and placed in the earthly paradise; and how Eve was created from his rib; how they were forbidden to eat of the tree of knowledge, but did eat, and thus sinned; and then clothed in garments of skin and expelled from paradise, they lived out their whole lives in great hardship and penance, deprived of the original justice which they had lost. Next I will use my intellect to reason about this in greater detail, and then use the will, as is described just above.*

Point Three: Use the same method on *the particular sin of anyone who has gone to hell because of one mortal sin; and further, of innumerable other persons who went there for fewer sins than I have committed.*

(Spiritual Exercises, 48, 50-52)

Commentary

All preparation for the kingdom of Christ must begin with sincere remorse of heart. Only as we recognize our sinfulness can we hope to be justified, like the tax collector praying in the Temple. With him, we should say with all the sincerity of our being: "God, be merciful to me a sinner!" (Luke 18:13).

If this cry is to rise sincerely from the depths of our souls, we must first desire to submit all our powers of judgment to God. Our limited ability to reason needs to be illuminated and prepared to grasp the mysterious reality of human sin. Only in this way will we be able to condemn sin as God wishes.

How can you cultivate this disposition of repentance? In prayer, try imagining yourself coming before the Lord like an employee who has been exposed as an embezzler and who now meets the employer who had put all his confidence in him. Or see yourself as a son or daughter who appears before their father after having betrayed him in a cowardly and shameful manner. Through these and other ways, you can arrive at a genuinely felt petition for shame and confusion over your sins.

If our feelings are not to be merely superficial, they must proceed from God's grace. But we can prepare ourselves by letting God's light shine on our minds and hearts to reveal the sad reality of sin. And when God offers us this revelation, we can accept his objective judgments without making excuses.

Here are a few points and Scripture passages on which to read and reflect. They can help you exercise your understanding in order to receive the light that comes from divine revelation.

For Reflection

Meditatively read 2 Peter 2:4-10. This passage shows how God responds when his creatures say, "I will not serve." Out of rebellious pride that wants to supplant God and occupy his place, they say, "We will be like God." Instead, divine judgment falls on them.

Since all of Scripture has been written for our benefit, we should reflect seriously on how we react to sin. We should stir up our will to desire and ask for the ability to adopt God's view. His is the only appropriate judgment regarding sin. As St. Augustine says: "Since we are already sinners, let us at least resemble God in this way: that we may despise what he despises. In this way you unite yourself with the will of God, when you despise in yourself what the One who made you hates" (*Sermon 19,3*).

What especially strikes you as you reflect on the sin of the fallen angels?

Meditatively read Genesis 3. Adam and Eve fell from friendship with God as a result of yielding to the serpent's temptations. In any sin there exists a complicity with evil spirits. Because of this, sin taints our deepest relationships—with the rest of creation, with other men and women, and above all with our Creator, whose original plan was to reach out to us in loving dialogue.

Genesis 3 reveals sin as a choice of immediate pleasure that obscures our faith in God's word, at least momentarily. This divine word impresses itself on us as our most serious obligation. Why, then, do we allow its future promise to be eclipsed by the allure of sin's immediate pleasure? The ugly truth is that sin always involves a substitution: the creature for the Creator. How ashamed and embarrassed I should be to discover this attitude in myself! How determined I should be to increase my hatred for the idolatry involved in all sin!

Sin represents the desire to liberate ourselves from God and overturn his ordering of the world, plunging us into the darkness of personal loneliness and exile. We fall into a slavery of our own seeking and are taken prisoner by our unbridled desires. Here are yet more reasons for shame and confusion: our absurd opposition to God, our seeking for slavery, and above all our situation of enmity with God. Only the divine Redeemer will be able to break the yoke that sin has laid on our backs.

Read Genesis 3 with particular attention to the points mentioned above. Which ones do you find especially relevant? Which areas and attitudes should you be praying about and working to change?

Meditatively read 1 Corinthians 6:9-10 and Galatians 5:19-21. As these passages point out, sin excludes us from the kingdom of God and brings eternal condemnation. "Do you not know that the unrighteous will not inherit the kingdom of God?" asks St. Paul (1 Corinthians 6:9). Our sins condemn us to be forever deprived of the joyful presence of God—to be definitively separated from him, eternally prevented from attaining the goal which is the most intimate aspiration of our existence.

St. Ignatius advises us to reflect on the fact that although people can condemn themselves through even a *single* sin, we have not yet been condemned in spite of our *many* sins. If one mortal sin is grounds for condemnation, how much we should appreciate God's mercy! He is allowing us the opportunity to repent and receive his forgiveness.

Read 1 Corinthians 6:9-10 and Galatians 5:19-21. Take some time to reflect on the gravity of sin and the dangers it entails. Consider writing a prayer that expresses your repentance and desire to hate sin the way God does.

Colloquy

St. Ignatius ends this meditation on sin with a colloquy, or prayer of dialogue. *Imagine Christ our Lord suspended on the cross before you, and converse with him* (*Spiritual Exercises*, 53). He urges us to ponder the great mystery of Jesus' sacrifice and to consider our response to it most seriously. We can approach Christ using words like these:

And so I come to the feet of Christ the Redeemer, crucified for our sins. Jesus, you are God made man. You are the Creator become a creature, who came from eternal life to be incarnated in human nature. You submitted yourself to time and space, to pain and death in order to die for my sins and reconcile me with the Father. You canceled my debt. You revoked the decree of condemnation that was hanging over me.

Guided by faith and as realistically as possible, I must now ask myself:
What has Christ done for me?
What have I done for Christ?
What should I do for Christ?

The Son of God "loved me and gave himself for me" (Galatians 2:20). I ask for the grace to know that I am eternally indebted to Christ for my redemption. May this realization move me to respond generously in love, as the Spirit suggests in my interior being.

Contrition

Words of St. Ignatius

The petition underlying this exercise is *to ask for growing and intense sorrow and tears for my sins*. St. Ignatius proposes various points for reflection as helps to this goal. Here are some of them:

- *I will call to memory all the sins of my life, looking at them year by year or period by period.* Ignatius has a practical suggestion for how to carry out this *court record of my sins:* namely, to recall *first, the locality or house where I lived; second, the associations which I had with others; third, the occupation I was pursuing.*

- *[I will] ponder these sins* and face the fact that they are evil and ugly.

- *I will reflect upon myself. . . . First, what am I when compared with all other human beings? Second, what are they when compared with all the angels and saints in paradise? Third, what is all of creation when compared with God? And then, I alone—what can I be? . . .*

- *I will consider who God is against whom I have sinned, by going through his attributes and comparing them with their opposites in myself: God's wisdom with my ignorance; God's omnipotence with my weakness; God's justice with my iniquity; God's goodness with my malice.*

- St. Ignatius' last point is *an exclamation of wonder* at God's patience, as manifested in his creation. *The angels: How is it that, although they are the swords of God's justice, they have borne with me, protected me, and prayed for me? The saints: How is it that they have interceded and prayed for me? Likewise, the heavens, the sun, the moon, the stars, and the elements; the fruits, birds, fishes, and animals. . . .*

The exercise ends with a *colloquy of mercy—conversing with God our Lord and thanking him for granting me life until now, and proposing, with his grace, amendment for the future.*

(Spiritual Exercises, 55-61)

For Reflection

As a preparation for this exercise, consider praying Psalm 51 or one of the other penitential psalms. Note your thoughts here.

Commentary

In light of God's objective judgment on human sin, we have come to feel shame and confusion over our sins and to utterly detest them. The next step is to acknowledge and accept our share of the blame for wounding and offending God, asking ardently for the grace of true sorrow, contrition, and tears for our own sins.

Through our sinful actions and omissions, each of us has introduced evil into the world. How difficult it is to recognize my sins as my own and to weep before God over the offenses by which I have wounded him! True contrition for my personal sin can only be a work of the grace of God, who has come to meet us. It is a victory of the light of his mercy over our darkness (1 John 1:6-10).

Without attempting a detailed review of all my past sins, I must try to see the reality of my sinful life in the light of God's holiness and judgment on sin. All the revulsion and shame I feel before the horrible reality of my sins, contemplated in the divine light, should be converted into sorrow and tears in the presence of Christ crucified, who offers himself to the eternal Father for my salvation.

- Following St. Ignatius' suggestion, it may help me to bring before Christ's holy gaze the settings where my sins took place: the houses where I have lived . . . the streets and places of work, rest, or recreation where I have spent time . . . all the places in which I lived as a child, an adolescent, an adult. . . . I will do this without fear or haste, resisting the feverish agitation to rush past this humiliating display of my sins. The wound may burn, but in Christ there is a remedy. (At this time, it is not so much a matter of a detailed examination of facts, but of trying to see my sinful reality in the light of the divine holiness.)

- St. Ignatius counsels that we should try to recognize the maliciousness and repulsiveness of sin in itself, considering that God forbids whatever is evil, ugly, and unworthy of his sons or daughters.

- I will benefit from reflecting on the infinitesimal smallness of my being. Today's interplanetary voyages give the human imagination some idea of the vastness of space. How small each individual person must be—one among billions on this grain of sand which is our planet. And Earth itself belongs to just one of the innumerable galaxies that make up the firmament! Who am I to offend God by my sin?

- I must prepare my soul for sincere contrition by realizing my complete ignorance in the face of God's omniscience and infinite wisdom. This will highlight the offense of preferring my own ways to his, my shadows to his light. And if I compare God's justice with my sin, I will see more clearly how great an insult sin is to God. By despising his infinite goodness, I have also rejected and betrayed his friendship.

- If I arrive at the point where I can see the truth about my sin, I who have received so much from God will have to wonder in astonishment: "How is it possible that the weight of divine justice has not already fallen upon me?"

Colloquy

Returning to the feet of Christ crucified, I will praise him for his infinite patience and mercy with me. I will offer to make amends for my evil past, as much as I am able, through a life dedicated to his divine pleasure. Christ is the reparation for my sin. What should I do for him?

For Reflection

Allow as much time as you need to move through each of the points in this exercise. Use this space to record reflections regarding:

- the "court record" of your sins (see page 37)
- the unworthiness of the sin

- God's greatness and human weakness
- how, by sinning, you have despised God

- the mercy of God, who "makes his sun rise on the evil and on the good, and sends rain on the just and on the unjust" (Matthew 5:45).

"I will sing of thy steadfast love, O LORD, for ever" (Psalm 89:1). This is the exclamation of the penitent heart: remorseful, humbled, and overflowing with gratitude.

If you have a copy of the *Spiritual Exercises*, this is a good moment to review the "Additional Directives" that St. Ignatius recommends. (*Spiritual Exercises*, 73-90).

Conversion

Words of St. Ignatius

Repeat Exercises one and two, on sin and contrition, paying special attention to the points where you had a deeper sense of consolation or desolation, or had a greater spiritual experience. Then, in three conversational prayers, or colloquies, ask for some specific gifts:

The First Colloquy will be with our Lady, that she may obtain for me from her Son and Lord grace for three things:

First, that I may feel an interior knowledge of my sins and also an abhorrence of them;
Second, that I may perceive the disorder in my actions, in order to detest them, amend myself, and put myself in order;
Third, that I may have a knowledge of the world, in order to detest it and rid myself of all that is worldly and vain. Then I will say a Hail Mary.

The Second Colloquy. I will make the same requests to the Son, asking him to obtain these graces for me from the Father. Then I will say the prayer Soul of Christ.

The Third Colloquy. I will address these same requests to the Father, asking that he himself, the eternal Lord, may grant me these graces. Then I will say an Our Father.

(Spiritual Exercises, 62-63)

Commentary

The three successive colloquies, or conversations, are meant to deepen and purify my understanding of my true position as a repentant sinner before Our Lord. The first is addressed to Our Lady so that she may intercede for me before her divine Son. The second is to Jesus Christ, our Mediator and Advocate before the Father (1 John 2:1-2). The third is to the Father himself. In this conversation, three graces are requested:

1. *Total abhorrence of all forms of sin.* This is not a mere mental affirmation of fact, but a conviction at the deepest core of my being. It must burn in me like a purifying fire that cleanses me of all that is incompatible with God's infinite holiness.

My hatred of sin must include even "small" sins. It is true that venial sins do not alienate us entirely from God, as mortal sins do. But venial sins direct us away from our goal and create a kind of fog between us and God; we begin to make compromises and become impervious to actual grace. Besides being an obstacle to spiritual development in Christ, venial sins are a clear danger to persevering in sanctifying grace. They are also an offense against God.

Venial sins affect our apostolic activity. Very often, they are the reason for the lack of fruitfulness we experience in our service to God.

2. *The grace to* feel *interiorly everything in me that is not directed towards* God. If one single ray of divine light were to shine through the window of my soul, how many "little foxes" I would see damaging my garden (Song of Songs 2:15)!

Half heartedness in my religious practices, my tendency to put off anything that does not appeal to me, the emptiness of my conversation, the thoughtless superficiality of my work, my inclination to speak without listening, my disorganized use of time, my instinctive favoritism, presumption, and self-aggrandizing, my emotional highs and lows, my resistance to things requiring effort, my difficulty in rising above myself. . . . Are these some of the things I would notice if the Lord let me see myself clearly? Would I see that even my most altruistic and religious actions have become stained by egotism?

To feel the disorder within me is the first step toward hating it. Then I can begin to struggle against it, receive correction, and amend my life.

3. *Spiritual sensitivity.* This will enable me to distinguish the signs and ordinary causes of disorder in the reality around me so that I will not be deceived by the world. Poisoned by the sin of the angels, of Adam, and by our own sins, the world has a wisdom which is not that of Christ (1 Corinthians 3:19). It proposes a hierarchy of values that run contrary to his.

The fallen world's evaluation ignores the authentic purposes for which created beings and things were made. It treats them as ends in themselves, as the sole or main objects of our desires. This disconnects them from their source and from their essential orientation towards God. Stripped of their specifically Christian significance, they lose their substance and become merely "vain and earthly" realities which cannot accomplish their mission for the glorification of God and the salvation of souls.

The world's promise of a leisurely and simple life is so seductive! In every area of my life, vanity, comfort, convenience reach out to attract me. "The fascination of wickedness obscures what is good" (Wisdom 4:12). How much I need the spiritual sensitivity to discern the subtle hollowness of reality and the work of "the father of lies" (John 8:44)!

In my prayer, I will ask to recognize the deception of the world that opposes Christ. I will ask for help to reject and avoid temptations to make myself over according to the world's agenda.

For Reflection

Review the present exercise, stopping to assimilate the feelings or insights that the Lord has communicated to you regarding the reality of sin in your life and your need to abhor and make amends for it. Which points do you especially keep in mind?

Deliberately and with fervent desire, ask for the three graces highlighted in this exercise as you turn to Our Lady, to Christ, and to the Father. You may find it helpful to write down your three requests in your own words.

As you reflect on sin and seek to arrive at a deeper response, try using some of these Scripture passages as a point of departure. Note any reflections that would be useful for further prayer.

Baruch 3:1-8. Sin as a form of exile, abandonment, distance from the Father's house.

Isaiah 5:1-8. Sin as ingratitude.

Job 9:1-20. Sin as insolence.

Psalm 51. This is the psalm known as the *Miserere*—an expression of lament, confidence, and consolation. You might pray it slowly, pausing to reflect on the significance of each word or phrase. St. Ignatius recommends and explains this method of prayer in the *Spiritual Exercises* (249-257).

With serenity, allow the attitudes of a repentant sinner to take root in you before the Lord. You have considered your sinful life as it appears to God's eyes rather than to the superficial gaze of people around you. Now you can love God with a new energy and passion grounded in reality! This prayer from St. Ignatius, the *Anima Christi*, or Soul of Christ, can help you express your love and intention:

Soul of Christ, sanctify me.
Body of Christ, save me.
Blood of Christ, inebriate me.
Water from the side of Christ, wash me.
Passion of Christ, strengthen me.
O good Jesus, hear me.
Within your wounds hide me.
Do not allow me to be separated from you.
From the malevolent enemy defend me.
In the hour of my death, call me,
and bid me come to you,
that with your saints I may praise you
forever and ever. Amen.

Words of St. Ignatius

Keep in mind the five steps St. Ignatius recommended for the daily examen:

1. *To give thanks to God our Lord for the benefits I have received.*
2. *To ask grace to know my sins and rid myself of them.*
3. *To ask an account of my soul from the hour of rising to the present examen, . . . first as to thoughts, then words, then deeds. . . .*
4. *To ask pardon of God our Lord for my faults.*
5. *To resolve, with his grace, to amend them.*
   Close with an Our Father.

(Spiritual Exercises, 43)

Commentary

In going through the *Spiritual Exercises*, we sometimes experience a tendency to focus in on ourselves. There is a danger here: We risk getting lost in a labyrinth of thoughts and being trapped within our own limitations and fantasies as we reflect over and over on the past.

Such an attitude is the very opposite of what we should aim for in these meditations on sin and repentance. It distracts us from the focal point of all Christian experience, which is Christ the Redeemer. Not by closing ourselves up in our own shadows will we reach our goal, but by opening ourselves to the light and grace that come from God! Only grace can illuminate the truth of this mysterious reality of sin in ourselves. Only grace can move us to remorse and to the authentic Christian repentance through which we are purified and renewed.

At this point in the *Exercises*, it is essential that we get accustomed to looking at our faults and sins with spiritual vision. We affirm our position before God and, with the eyes of the soul, we find ourselves in the presence of Christ, whose divine gaze penetrates our hearts and innermost being—this is to bring light where once there was darkness. It is to recognize in ourselves the ongoing work of salvation.

Viewed this way, the examination of conscience is a very useful exercise which situates us in the center of this Christian reality. We enter into the depths of our soul, but not with the purpose of becoming self-satisfied or scrupulously self-reproachful for our failings. Rather, we seek to find ourselves again in faith and to recognize Christ's saving action at work in us through the Spirit—all before the invisible gaze of the Father, who inspires our every initiative for good.

Scripture tells us that the Father directs everything "for good with those who love him" (Romans 8:28). But it is one thing to know this, and another to recognize it in the concrete events of each day. Can you believe that God is working today, wherever you are right now, in the important and in the trivial, the pleasurable and the painful, the victories and the tragedies? The daily examen sees everything in this light. It therefore makes sense to begin it, as St. Ignatius advises, by thanking the Lord even for those things that have caused you pain and suffering. Everything can be transformed for good, even the most deplorable offenses and betrayals, when we turn in trust to the divine mercy.

This attitude of trusting openness before the Lord will help you to discover the roots of your failings. Our interest here is not so much our faults in themselves, but rather the interior disorders and afflictions from which they spring—the deep-seated attitudes and dynamics which nurture them and set them in motion. Christ the Light reveals all these twists and turnings of the heart. His word is living and active, "piercing to the division of soul and spirit" and "discerning the thoughts and intentions of the heart" (Hebrews 4:12).

We participate in this aspect of Christ's mission as we learn to approach our daily review without fear, anxiety, or obsession. We join ourselves to Christ's judgment on the world—first of all, as we discover sin's inroads within ourselves. We offer our cooperation in Jesus' mission of casting out "the ruler of this world"—the prince of darkness and father of lies—by the mysterious power of the cross (John 12:31-32).

With these things in mind, always seek to approach your daily review in a spirit of *sincere sorrow and conversion*, asking for *help and redemption* from the only One who can grant them. You will find healing for your wounds in the gentle hands of this divine Physician. He knows how to treat them without further irritating them, since he alone sees them as they really are. Take heart, then, and hear Jesus' invitation to continue your struggle against the kingdom of darkness within.

As you do this, your contrition will be genuinely Christian. Your resolve to improve will be revitalized again and again—even as you have repeated experiences of your own inconstancy, failings, defects, and incomplete appropriation of Christ's redemption. Undiscouraged, you can press ahead in the spirit of Simon Peter: Lord, "at your word I will let down the nets" (Luke 5:5)!

For Reflection

Scripture often recommends that we examine our inner selves in God's presence and points to various results. What thoughts do the following passages inspire in you?

"Let a man examine himself, and so eat of the bread and drink of the cup" (1 Corinthians 11:28).

"So whether we are at home or away, we make it our aim to please him. For we must all appear before the judgment seat of Christ, so that each one may receive good or evil, according to what he has done in the body. Therefore, knowing the fear of the Lord, we persuade men; but what we are is known to God, and I hope it is known also to your conscience" (2 Corinthians 5:9-11).

"Examine yourselves, to see whether you are holding to your faith. Test yourselves. Do you not realize that Jesus Christ is in you?—unless indeed you fail to meet the test!" (2 Corinthians 13:5).

"For the word of God is living and active, sharper than any two-edged sword, piercing to the division of soul and spirit, of joints and marrow, and discerning the thoughts and intentions of the heart. And before him no creature is hidden, but all are open and laid bare to the eyes of him with whom we have to do" (Hebrews 4:12-13).

As part of your reflection, take some time to think about your daily examen. The following questions may reveal areas for improvement:

Do I acknowledge that my sins are an obstacle to intimacy with God? Or is my relationship with the Lord merely lukewarm because I persuade myself that "I haven't really sinned very much"? What can I learn from the woman about whom Jesus said: "Therefore I tell you, her sins, which are many, are forgiven, for she loved much; but he who is forgiven little, loves little" (Luke 7:47)?

Have I allowed my daily review to become centered on me in a way that obscures my focus on God? What can I do to change this?

Have I abandoned that loving attitude of *vigilance* which the gospel recommends? Do I need to stir myself to more fervent devotion and love of the Lord?

Have I allowed myself to become too busy for a regular examination of conscience? Do I appreciate it as a valuable way of discovering and opening myself to Christ's saving work as it unfolds for *me*, in the specific circumstances of my daily life?

Discernment of Spirits

Very often, people who are going through the *Spiritual Exercises* find that they experience an interior movement of the soul in one direction or the other. Sometimes they feel fervent, enlightened, and drawn toward what is good. At other times, they feel restless, troubled, and tempted toward what is evil. It is important to recognize such feelings, because they help or hinder the process of turning more seriously to God. This is why St. Ignatius, as an expert guide of souls, offered some helpful rules and guidelines on this subject.

If you have a copy of the *Spiritual Exercises*, this is a good time to read about "discernment of spirits"—that is, about identifying and dealing with these inner "motions" of the soul (313-327). These norms were written mainly for spiritual directors, but even without one you can benefit from this advice. Ignatius intended it to be useful for the spiritual life in general, not just for the duration of the *Exercises*.

Words of St. Ignatius

Ignatius' first and most universally applicable rules of discernment deal with two opposites, which he calls "consolation" and "desolation."

Consolation . . . *occurs when some interior motion is caused within the soul through which it comes to be inflamed with love of its Creator and Lord. As a result it can love no created thing on the face of the earth in itself, but only in the Creator of them all.*

Similarly, this consolation is experienced when the soul sheds tears which move it to love for its Lord—whether they are tears of grief for its own sins, or about the Passion of Christ our Lord, or about other matters directly ordered to his service and praise.

Finally, under the word consolation I include every increase in hope, faith, and charity, and every interior joy which calls and attracts one toward heavenly things and to the salvation of one's soul, by bringing it tranquility and peace in its Creator and Lord.

Desolation is the contrary of consolation, says Ignatius. *For example, obtuseness of soul, turmoil within it, an impulsive motion towards low and earthly things, or disquiet from various agitations and* *temptations. These move one toward lack of faith and leave one without hope and without love. One is completely listless, tepid, and unhappy, and feels separated from our Creator and Lord.*

For just as consolation is contrary to desolation, so the thoughts which arise from consolation are likewise contrary to those which spring from desolation.

(Spiritual Exercises, 316-317)

For Reflection

Have you experienced "consolation," as St. Ignatius describes it here? How did it affect you?

What about "desolation"? How did you deal with it?

Are you aware of either of these "motions" tugging at you right now? How can you tell?

Advice for Good Times and for Bad

Words of St. Ignatius

Always practical, St. Ignatius offers down-to-earth help for making the most of the good times and getting through the bad.

One who is in consolation should consider how he or she will act in future desolation, and store up new strength for that time.

One who is in consolation ought to humble and abase herself or himself as much as possible, and reflect on how little she or he is worth in time of desolation when that grace or consolation is absent.

Not surprisingly, St. Ignatius offers more counsel to people who are experiencing desolation—first of all, a warning. During such a period, he says, *one should never make a change. Instead, one should remain firm and constant in the resolutions and in the decision which one had on the day before the desolation, or in a decision in which one was during a previous time of consolation.*

For just as the good spirit is chiefly the one who guides and counsels us in times of consolation, so it is the evil spirit who does this in time of desolation. By following his counsels we can never find the way to a right decision.

But this warning against changing our previous resolutions doesn't mean that we can't take any new steps. On the contrary! *It is very profitable to make vigorous changes in ourselves against the desolation, for example, by insisting more on prayer, meditation, earnest self-examination, and some suitable way of doing penance.*

St. Ignatius also points out that we should never think ourselves abandoned. Rather, *we should think that the Lord has left us to our own powers in order to test us, so that we may prove ourselves by resisting the various agitations and temptations of the enemy. For we can do this with God's help, which always remains available, even if we do not clearly perceive it. Indeed, . . . he still supplies sufficient grace for our eternal salvation.*

Patience is *the counterattack* to desolation, which will eventually yield to our diligent efforts against it. *One should remember that after a while the consolation will return again.*

(Spiritual Exercises, 323-324, 318-321)

For Reflection

St. Ignatius identifies three chief causes of desolation (*Spiritual Exercises*, 322). Look them over and then share your thoughts about them with the Lord:

Reason 1: We ourselves are tepid, lazy, or negligent in our spiritual exercises. Thus the spiritual consolation leaves us because of our own faults.

Reason 2: The desolation is meant to test how much we are worth and how far we will extend ourselves in the service and praise of God, even without much repayment by way of consolations and increased graces.

Reason 3: The desolation is meant to give us a true recognition and understanding, so that we may perceive interiorly that we cannot by ourselves bring on or retain great devotion, intense love, tears, or any other spiritual consolation, but that all these are a gift and grace from God our Lord; and further, to prevent us from building our nest in a house which belongs to Another, by puffing up our minds with pride or vainglory through which we attribute to ourselves the devotion or other features of spiritual consolation.

Know Your Enemy

Words of St. Ignatius

"Know your enemy" is classic advice for anyone engaged in warfare. St. Ignatius' insights into Satan's wiles and tactics provide help for our spiritual battle against the powers of darkness. They seem to be the fruit of his own experience, along with traditional Christian wisdom.

Do not yield an inch, Ignatius warns. *The enemy is weak when faced by firmness but strong in the face of acquiescence. . . .*

[He] characteristically weakens, loses courage, and flees with his temptations when the person engaged in spiritual endeavors stands bold and unyielding against the enemy's temptations and goes diametrically against them. But if, in contrast, that person begins to fear and lose courage in the face of the temptations, there is no beast on the face of the earth as fierce as the enemy of human nature when he is pursuing his damnable intention with his surging malice.

Similarly the enemy acts like a ***false lover,*** *insofar as he tries to remain secret and undetected. For such a scoundrel, speaking with evil intent and trying to seduce the daughter of a good father or the wife of a good husband, wants his words and solicitations to remain secret. But he is deeply displeased when the daughter reveals his deceitful words and evil design to her father, or the wife to her husband. For he easily infers that he cannot succeed in the design he began.*

In a similar manner, when the enemy of human nature turns his wiles and persuasions upon an upright person, he intends and desires them to be received and kept in secrecy. But when the person reveals them to his or her good confessor or some other spiritual person who understands the enemy's deceits and malice, he is grievously disappointed. For he quickly sees that he cannot succeed in the malicious project he began, because his manifest deceptions have been detected.

To use still another comparison, the enemy acts like a ***military commander*** *who is attempting to conquer and plunder his objective. The captain and leader of an army on campaign sets up his camp, studies the strength and structure of a fortress, and then attacks at its weakest point.*

In the same way, the enemy of human nature prowls around and from every side probes all our theological, cardinal, and moral virtues. Then at the point where he finds us weakest and most in need in regard to our eternal salvation, there he attacks and tries to take us.

(Spiritual Exercises, 325-327)

For Reflection

Which parts of St. Ignatius' advice especially relate to your experience? How might you apply his insights in your current spiritual battles?

St. Ignatius offers counsels that evoke Scripture's portrayal of the devil and his snares, as well as the victory Christ offers to those who stand firm. After inviting the Holy Spirit to guide your thoughts, use a few Scripture verses to reflect on these themes.

"Be sober, be watchful. Your adversary the devil prowls around like a roaring lion, seeking some one to devour. Resist him, firm in your faith, knowing that the same experience of suffering is required of your brotherhood throughout the world" (1 Peter 5:8-9).

"[The devil] was a murderer from the beginning, and has nothing to do with the truth, because there is no truth in him. When he lies, he speaks according to his own nature, for he is a liar and the father of lies" (John 8:44).

"For we are not contending against flesh and blood, but against the principalities, against the powers, against the world rulers of this present darkness, against the spiritual hosts of wickedness in the heavenly places. Therefore take the whole armor of God, that you may be able to withstand in the evil day, and having done all, to stand" (Ephesians 6:12-13).

"Now is the judgment of this world, now shall the ruler of this world be cast out; and I, when I am lifted up from the earth, will draw all men to myself" (John 12:31-32).

"Submit yourselves therefore to God. Resist the devil and he will flee from you." (James 4:7)

"Again Jesus spoke to them, saying, 'I am the light of the world; he who follows me will not walk in darkness, but will have the light of life'" (John 8:12).

Know Yourself

Words of St. Ignatius

The spiritual battle requires self-knowledge. After all, we have an enemy who cunningly adapts his tactics to fit our basic orientation and weaknesses.

In the case of persons who are going from one mortal sin to another, the enemy ordinarily proposes to them apparent pleasures. He makes them imagine delights and pleasures of the senses, in order to hold them fast and plunge them deeper into their sins and vices.

But with persons of this type, the good spirit uses a contrary procedure. Through their good judgment on problems of morality he stings their consciences with remorse.

In the case of persons who are earnestly purging away their sins, and who are progressing from good to better in the service of God our Lord, the procedure used is the opposite of that described above. For in this case it is characteristic of the evil spirit to cause gnawing anxiety, to sadden, and to set up obstacles. In this way he unsettles these persons by false reasons aimed at preventing their progress.

But with persons of this type it is characteristic of the good spirit to stir up courage and strength, consolations, tears, inspirations, and tranquility. He makes things easier and eliminates all obstacles, so that the persons may move forward in doing good.

(Spiritual Exercises, 314-315)

For Reflection

Which tactics of the enemy am I most susceptible to?

How can I strengthen my defenses and increase my vigilance against temptation?

A Meditation on Death

"Remember the end of your life, and then you will never sin." (Sirach 7:36)

Commentary

Why is death the subject for a meditation? It can seem so morbid and depressing. And yet, as St. Ignatius and many other spiritual writers have known, thinking about our mortality can open our eyes to the truth—about what is truly worth pursuing in life, about what is deceptively attractive and leads to the death of the soul. It can help us to untangle our hearts from our disordered attachments to the things of this world. Then, trusting in God but appropriately sobered by knowing what hangs in the balance, we can carry out the command to "work out your own salvation with fear and trembling" (Philippians 2:12).

Death is an unmasking of sin and, as Scripture tells us, a participation in the death of Adam. "Sin came into the world through one man and death through sin, and so death spread to all men because all men sinned" (Romans 5:12). But for Christians, it is also a participation in the Lord's death, through which we were redeemed: "Do you not know that all of us who have been baptized into Christ Jesus were baptized into his death? We were buried therefore with him by baptism into death, so that as Christ was raised from the dead by the glory of the Father, we too might walk in newness of life" (6:3-4). Even in death, then, we have cause to rejoice, "for as in Adam all die, so also in Christ shall all be made alive" (1 Corinthians 15:22).

In his teaching, Jesus evoked vivid images when he spoke about human death. Similarly, without inducing fright or terror, we can benefit from being vivid in our meditation on death. One approach is to reflect on the points in this meditation from the perspective you are likely to have when you find yourself at the moment of death.

Begin with the preparatory prayer (it is found on page 28 and is number 46 of the *Spiritual Exercises*). Recall that God is with you as you begin this meditation. In particular, ask for the grace to receive the fruits which the Lord intended when he spoke of death. Imagine how sincerely you would ask and listen if you were on your deathbed or knew you were going to die tomorrow! Seek to arrive at that degree of attentiveness. Then, reflect on the following points, moving through them at your own pace. Use the space provided for noting thoughts to which you may want to return.

For Reflection

Be prepared. Resist the tendency to think of death as something that will not happen to you. Jesus insisted that we see death as always present on the horizon: "You also must be ready; for the Son of man is coming at an unexpected hour" (Luke 12:40). The parable of the foolish virgins makes the same point (Matthew 25:1-13). Following Jesus, St. Paul and St. Peter also urge us to watchful hope (1 Thessalonians 5:2-8; 1 Peter 1:13).

Death reminds me that I am not self-sufficient. I serve the Lord, and it is crucial that he find me faithful in his service when he returns (Luke 12:37). I must "watch and pray" because I know neither the day nor the hour of my Master's return (Matthew 26:41; 24:42-44)—or of my own death.

Treasure that lasts. Sports, daydreams, entertainment, wealth, fame, comfort, debate and controversy—how drawn we are to such things! How easily we become attached to them and pursue them as idols! Jesus warned against this vain and disastrous frivolity. Recall his parable of the rich miser who thought he could rest secure because his harvest had been abundant. How his anxieties vanished as he contemplated the heaps of grain in his barns! "Take your ease, eat, drink, be merry," he told himself. But God's message to him was entirely different: "Fool! This night your soul is required of you; and the things you have prepared, whose will they be?" (Luke 12:16-20).

Where have I placed my trust? What sort of treasure have I stored up for myself? What do I really rely on? To whom will this treasure go when I die?

Chasing shadows? At the moment of death, God removes us from everything to which our hearts have become inordinately attached. When we arrive at this hour of truth, how pointless these attachments will appear! We have sinned on account of such small things! We have lost so much over so little!

Similarly, death separates us from things and reveals the radical distinction between persons and things. We are no longer able to identify with work, positions, honors, titles, talents, health, or other realities that are not our true selves. Sometimes, only the thought of death can open our eyes to this dangerous and fatal identification.

"What has our arrogance profited us?" say the wicked in the Book of Wisdom, once they realize their foolishness. "And what good has our boasted wealth brought us? All those things have vanished like a shadow, and like a rumor that passes by. . ." (Wisdom 5:8-9). What about me? What will *I* say when *I* am at the point of death?

A clearer perspective. By meditating on our death, we can come to see life in better perspective, as from across eternity's shore. "Everything I see with the eyes of my body is like a dream, like a trifle," said St. Teresa of Avila, after one of her experiences of deep prayer. "Those who truly love God and who have forsaken the things of this life should die more peacefully" (*Life*, chapter 38). From this other shore, we discover not only what is worthless, but also what is truly of value in the eyes of God.

Jesus' words tell me what God values: "I was hungry and you gave me food, I was thirsty and you gave me drink, I was a stranger and you welcomed me, I was naked and you clothed me, I was sick and you visited me, I was in prison and you came to me" (Matthew 25:35-36). Are my values like God's?

Diligent labor. Work "while it is day," Jesus said. "Night comes, when no one can work" (John 9:4). Our faithful labors for the Lord in this life should be spurred on by a healthy remembrance of death. "Do not allow those who work for temporal things to have more care and diligence than you for eternal things," St. Ignatius warned in one of his letters (*The Letter on Perfection*).

Jesus said to "lay up for yourselves treasures in heaven, where neither moth nor rust consumes and where thieves do not break in and steal" (Matthew 6:20). Am I doing this?

Why delay? Death happens to us only once. Where the tree falls is where it will lie (Ecclesiastes 11:3). During life, we decide where we will be after death: either with God or apart from God.

Why not deprive myself now of every dead weight that will hinder me at the decisive hour? The more I have been attached to these things, the more it will cost me to detach myself from them later. "For me, to live is Christ, and to die is gain," said St. Paul (Philippians 1:21). Can I say the same? Do I wish to?

"The pain of living forever without Him and the desire to enjoy the true life should temper our fear of death" (St. Teresa of Avila, *Life*, chapter 21).

You might find it fruitful to extend this exercise by meditating on these additional Scripture verses:

- about loving God wholeheartedly: Luke 10:27
- about purity of intention: Matthew 6:1-19

- about lukewarmness: Revelation 2:1-5; 3:14-19
- about distinguishing the true value of things, as revealed in the light of the moment of death: Luke 12:15-20; 1 Corinthians 7:29-32; Sirach 41:1-14; Philippians 1:20-26
- about divine judgment: Daniel 12:1-3; Revelation 20:11-15; Matthew 25:31-46; 1 Corinthians 3:13.

A Meditation on Hell

When we begin to consent to sin frequently and easily, we slow down in our spiritual progress and may forget our goal entirely. This very real and serious danger often develops when we reject and lose our fear of sin. "I want to act out of love, not fear," we tell ourselves. Then we let this love grow weaker and weaker, until at last our infidelity causes it to disappear.

What a priceless grace it is to perceive simultaneously the heights of God's love and the depths of sin's abyss and of our own frailty! Anyone who has had this experience turns spontaneously to the Lord and cries out to be fortified at all costs, so as not to fall: "Lead us not into temptation" (Matthew 6:13)! Healthy fear can act as the strengthening agent we need here, as Pope Pius XII once explained: "Since our hearts, disturbed as they are at times by the lower appetites, do not always respond to motives of love, it is also extremely helpful to let consideration and contemplation of the justice of God provoke us on occasion to salutary fear, and guide us from there to Christian humility, repentance and amendment" (*Mediator Dei*: AAS 39, 1947, 535; English trans. by The America Press, 1961, 26).

Adopting this perspective will help you derive the greatest benefit from St. Ignatius' meditation on hell.

Words of St. Ignatius

Following the usual *preparatory prayer*, ask God for the specific grace at which this meditation aims: *an interior sense of the pain suffered by the damned, so that if through my faults I should forget the love of the Eternal Lord, at least the fear of those pains will serve to keep me from falling into sin.*

Apply your mind to the "composition of place." *Here it will be to see in imagination the length, breadth, and depth of hell.* Ignatius offers "points" for engaging the senses when contemplating the Bible's expressions about hell.

Point One: to see with the eyes of the imagination the huge fires and, so to speak, the souls within the bodies full of fire.

Point Two: In my imagination I will hear the wailing, the shrieking, the cries, and the blasphemies against our Lord and all his saints.

Point Three: By my sense of smell I will perceive the smoke, the sulphur, the filth, and the rotting things.

Point Four: By my sense of taste I will experience the bitter flavors of hell: tears, sadness, and the worm of conscience.

Point Five: By my sense of touch, I will feel how the flames touch the souls and burn them.

Remember that you are doing this exercise in the presence of a God who loves you and desires your good. Talk it over with him now, in the way St. Ignatius suggests:

I will carry on a colloquy with Christ our Lord. I will call to mind the souls who are in hell: Some are there because they did not believe in Christ's coming; and others who, although they believed, did not act according to his commandments. . . .

Thereupon I will thank Christ because he has not, by ending my life, let me fall. . . . I will also thank him because he has shown me, all through my life up to the present moment, so much pity and mercy. I will close with an Our Father.

(Spiritual Exercises, 65-71)

Commentary

Save Me, O Lord. In this meditation, St. Ignatius advises us to use our imagination and apply our senses so as to understand the reality to which Jesus pointed when he warned about eternal condemnation. If we open ourselves to the intense love of Jesus, we will beg to have some feeling—that is, some interior sense—of hell's pains to keep us from falling into sin again. So let our heart's cry become: "Never permit me to be separated from you, Lord!"

To prepare ourselves for receiving the grace of this exercise, we must take seriously the warnings made repeatedly by the Lord in his preaching and in the written word inspired by the Holy Spirit. God used these terms and images to communicate the reality of hell, and we must allow them to sink in and produce the healthy effects for which he intends them. So let us reflect on what Scripture has to say about hell.

Try to see before your eyes: "the outer darkness" into which those who are condemned must go (Matthew 8:12) . . . "the unquenchable fire" (Mark 9:43) . . . the great and uncrossable chasm that cuts off the condemned from the saved (Luke 16:26) . . . the horrible sensation of terror of the wicked, who are "shaken with dreadful fear" (Wisdom 5:2).

Allow yourself to hear and be touched by the desperate cries of those who have finally come to see—but too late—that they "strayed from the way of truth": "What has our arrogance profited us? And what good has our boasted wealth brought us? All those things have vanished like a shadow" (Wisdom 5:6,8-9).

In your meditation on hell, apply the sense of smell. Imagine the odor that must arise from sin. Consider the pool of burning fire and sulfur mentioned in the Book of Revelation: the beast and false prophet were thrown into it (19:20; 20:10), and "the smoke of their torment goes up for ever and ever" (14:11).

Taste and feel the pains of hell: the bitterness and weeping (Matthew 13:42) . . . the "gnashing of teeth" (Matthew 13:50) . . . the worms that never die (Mark 9:48). Try to imagine the hunger to be experienced by those who now live with full stomachs, and the weeping of those who now laugh (Luke 6:25). Seek that spiritual understanding which moved the prophet Jeremiah to exclaim: "Know and see that it is evil and bitter for you to forsake the LORD your God" (Jeremiah 2:19).

Lord, do not permit that I become separated from you! May my flesh burn with a holy fear of you! Help me to escape the eternal fire and "nether gloom of darkness" (Jude 13).
May I never choose to follow "those who do not obey the gospel of our Lord Jesus" and who will therefore "suffer the punishment of eternal destruction and exclusion from the presence of the LORD and from the glory of his might" (2 Thessalonians 1:8-9).

Use this space for notes and reflections.

Thank You, Lord! Only by perceiving the magnitude of condemnation can I begin to get some idea of the magnitude of Christ's redemption. Only as I recognize the eternal fate from which Christ has saved me will I be truly grateful for what he gained for me at the price of his blood and his death on the cross. Then, too, I will better understand the zeal of Christ our Savior and stir up my own enthusiasm to do everything I can to follow him and help others avoid the road to perdition. "Enter by the narrow gate; for the gate is wide and the way is easy, that leads to ruin, and those who enter by it are many" (Matthew 7:13).

In grateful response to Christ's burning love for me, I will make a colloquy with my Lord, placed on the cross for my salvation. I will pour out my heart before this Lord of mercy, the center of all of history, who sustains my being. Even now, he saves me from becoming one of those who do not believe in his return. He gives me a chance to escape the ranks of those who once believed but were condemned because they never changed their lives in accordance with God's commandments. Jesus still offers me the possibility of recognizing my situation and taking refuge in his infinite mercy.

What shall I offer to the Lord in return for his patience with me? My eternal debt of gratitude and friendship will be expressed in the Eucharist's celebration: "Through him, with him, in him … all glory."

For Reflection

Spend as much time as you need for this exercise, looking up Scripture references and reflecting on them as the Spirit leads you. Consider praying Psalm 30 in your concluding conversation with the Lord, as an expression of thanks for his saving love.

Penance and the Eucharist

At this point in your journey through the *Spiritual Exercises*, it would be especially appropriate to express your gratitude to God by receiving the Sacraments of Reconciliation and the Eucharist. You might find this an especially good opportunity for making a general confession of the sins of your past life, as well as for asking yourself whether or not regular confession has the place it should in your spiritual life.

As you prepare your confession, be sure to meditate on God's mercy. Prayerfully reading Luke 15 will help you in this. Other passages that speak of sin and pardon, death and life: John 20:19-23; 15:1-8; Romans 12:5-8; 14:7-16.

Follow up your confession with a particularly vibrant and well-prepared participation in the Sacrament of the Holy Eucharist.

With

him

Step Two

the call and the response

A Meditation on the Call

"You go into the vineyard too." (Matthew 20:7)

The call of the eternal King and Lord of the universe, Jesus Christ, to each and every one of us, is no myth or fantasy. The apostles and disciples who heard his voice in Palestine lived out this call in history. They were slow to recognize fully the deeper reality of the kingdom of Christ, initially interpreting it in terms of temporal advantages and prestige. Finally, though, they understood it in the light of the Holy Spirit. Then they were able to rejoice at having been found worthy to suffer insults for the glory of Christ.

In the light of this same Spirit, these first followers were able to understand and transmit the universal significance of the call of Christ—the meaning of the deeds and words of the incarnate Son of God, who redeemed us by his death on the cross and calls us to follow him. As they affirmed, God's plan was not only to rescue us from darkness, but to place us in the kingdom of his Son (Colossians 1:13). Jesus, the firstborn of all creation, has been made the first fruits of all who are saved. "For as in Adam all die, so also in Christ shall all be made alive" (1 Corinthians 15:22). All who believe in him receive with him "power to become children of God" (John 1:12)—sons and daughters in the Son—chosen by God the Father "to be conformed to the image of his Son, in order that he might be the first-born among many brethren" (Romans 8:29).

When Christ the eternal King and universal Lord sends his personal call to each one of us to follow him, we are summoned to be coworkers in carrying out this supreme plan of the Father. It is to stir our enthusiasm and appreciation for this mission that St. Ignatius proposed the following meditation on "the call of the temporal king, as an aid toward contemplating the life of the eternal King."

Words of St. Ignatius

Following the usual *preparatory prayer*, begin by mentally "composing" the place which will set the scene for this meditation. *Here it will be to see with the eyes of the imagination the synagogues, villages, and castles through which Christ our Lord passed as he preached.*

I ask our Lord for a particular grace: *that I may not be deaf to his call, but ready and diligent to accomplish his most holy will.*

Then I prayerfully consider each of the following points:
Point One. I will place before my mind a human king, chosen by God our Lord himself, whom all Christian princes and all Christian persons reverence and obey.

Point Two. I will observe how this king speaks to all his people, saying, "My will is to conquer the whole land of the infidels. Hence, whoever wishes to come with me has to be content with the same food I eat, and the drink, and the clothing which I wear, and so forth. So too each one must labor with me during the day, and keep watch in the night, and so on, so that later each may have a part with me in the victory, just as each has shared in the toil."

Point Three. I will consider what good subjects ought to respond to a king so generous and kind; and how, consequently, if someone did not answer his call, he would be scorned and upbraided by everyone and accounted as an unworthy knight.

Part two of this exercise is to apply the above parable of a temporal king to Christ, according to the same three points:

Point One. If we give consideration to such a call from the temporal king to his subjects, how much more worthy of our consideration it is to gaze upon Christ our Lord, the eternal King, and all the world assembled before him. He calls to them all, and to each person in particular he says: "My will is to conquer the whole world and all my enemies, and thus to enter into the glory of my Father. Therefore, whoever wishes to come with me must labor with me, so that through following me in the pain he or she may follow me also in the glory."

Point Two. Reflect that all those who have judgment and reason will offer themselves wholeheartedly for this labor.

Point Three. Those who desire to show greater devotion and to distinguish themselves in total service to their eternal King and universal Lord, will not only offer their persons for the labor, but go further still. They will work against their human sensitivities and against their carnal and worldly love, and they will make offerings of greater worth and moment, and say:

"Eternal Lord of all things, I make my offering, with your favor and help. I make it in the presence of your infinite Goodness, and of your glorious Mother, and of all the holy men and women in your heavenly court. I wish and desire, and it is my deliberate decision, provided only that it is for your greater service and praise, to imitate you in bearing all injuries and affronts, and any poverty, actual as well as spiritual, if your Most Holy Majesty wishes to choose and receive me into such a life and state."

(Spiritual Exercises, 91-98)

For Reflection

You may also want to reflect on Jesus' words to his disciples:

"If any man would come after me, let him deny himself and take up his cross and follow me. For whoever would save his life will lose it, and whoever loses his life for my sake will find it. For what will it profit a man, if he gains the whole world and forfeits his life? Or what shall a man give in return for his life? For the Son of man is to come with his angels in the glory of his Father, and then he will repay every man for what he has done" (Matthew 16:24-27).

Commentary

The moment has arrived to meditate seriously on your own personal call. At the end of your meditation on sin, you came before Christ on the cross. Full of desire and generosity, humbled and overcome before the love of Jesus crucified for you, you asked: What ought I to do for Christ? Now is the time to respond to that question.

This exercise on the call of the eternal King must be founded on the concrete actions of the historical Christ, as transmitted and illuminated through the action of the Spirit in the apostles and in the Church. The Christ who traveled over the roads and preached in the town squares, synagogues, and fields of Palestine is the Lord of the universe. He still calls, acting intimately and powerfully in the life of each person who opens himself or herself to his revealed word.

Throughout this exercise, ask the Lord repeatedly to help you be quick and diligent to accomplish his most holy will—not deaf to the divine call.

St. Ignatius proposes meditating on a parable that compares the call of Christ with another call. Suppose, for example, that a valiant general—someone who is a friend of all and has the best of human qualities—calls his officers together to discuss a dangerous mission that is crucial for the safety of many people. Imagine him addressing the officers like this: "Men, this is going to be difficult, but it has to be done. I'm warning you: Anybody who follows me on this mission will have to put up with the same difficulties I'll be facing: the same rough paths, watchful nights, hard work, and daily struggles. But if you share the hardships with me, you'll have a share in the victory, too. What about it? Can I count on you?"

If this proposal came from a commander who was well liked and highly esteemed, how do you think the soldiers would respond? Wouldn't any soldier who refused to follow such a good leader on such a worthy mission be reviled and seen as cowardly?

For Reflection

If you prefer, make up another parable by imagining a similar scene with other kinds of characters. Just make sure that whatever story you imagine involves an outstanding leader and a most noble enterprise—something it would be shameful and cowardly to refuse to join in. Perhaps a father or mother who asks their children to help the family through a difficult situation, or a researcher who needs coworkers for a project that demands sacrifice.

Commentary

Now, we compare the call featured in our parable with Christ's call to each and every one of us in particular. This will highlight the fact that the divine call is much more worthy of our consideration than any other call.

In this case, our leader could not possibly be more good, noble, generous, self-sacrificing, or understanding. Likewise, the mission could hardly be more sublime or beneficial for all of humanity, or more glorious either for the Lord or for ourselves: *My will*, Christ says, *is to conquer the whole world and, when all my enemies have been subjected, to enter into the glory of my Father. Therefore, whoever would wish to come after me must work as I do, and suffer as I do, so that following me in toil, he may also follow me in glory* (*Spiritual Exercises*, 95).

Someone might protest that St. Ignatius isn't directly quoting Scripture when he imagines Christ saying such words. And yet, it is not misguided or "medieval" to imagine such a scene. Scripture itself suggests it: Christ "must reign until he has put all his enemies under his feet. The last enemy to be destroyed is death. For God has put all things in subjection under his feet. . . . When all things are subjected to him, then the Son himself will also be subjected to him who put all things under him, that God may be everything to every one" (1 Corinthians 15:25-27,28).

Through his life and words, Jesus explains how these battles for the kingdom are to be fought and how his enemies are to be overcome. The kingdom is Jesus himself, above all, along with those who share in it by acting as he does, living according to the Father's plan and will. The issue, therefore, is *holiness*. This is to be realized in the fulfillment of the divine plan to gather each person and all creation into Jesus. Everything must be directed towards Jesus, working and struggling with him and like him.

How important it is to consider the dignity of this undertaking! But above all, in your meditation, let yourself be attracted and fascinated by the person of Christ. The more you know and love this best of leaders, the better prepared you will be to go forward with him and struggle like him.

As you consider Christ and his call, you must naturally decide with your *reason* to offer yourself completely for his mission. Not only that, you should ask to *feel* in your heart some of the generosity that Christ showed when he saved you from eternal condemnation at the price of his own blood. This will help to stir up your most noble sentiments. With full awareness, you will resolve to surrender yourself totally to Jesus in an unconditional offering that will determine the remaining course of your whole life.

How many of those whom the Church has already declared saints or "blesseds" made this exercise in the past and responded to the call of the Lord! The self-offering that St. Ignatius proposes here made such an impression on Blessed John XXIII that he wrote it down so that he could repeat it every day. Read through it again slowly, as your own response to the risen Christ:

Eternal Lord of all things, I make my offering, with your favor and help. I make it in the presence of your infinite Goodness, and of your glorious Mother, and of all the holy men and women in your heavenly court. I wish and desire, and it is my deliberate decision, provided only that it is for your greater service and praise, to imitate you in bearing all injuries and affronts, and any poverty, actual as well as spiritual, if your Most Holy Majesty desires to choose and receive me into such a life and state (*Spiritual Exercises*, 98).

The Lord is present with you now. He sees you, accepts you as you are, and loves you with an unconditional love. Christ is calling you, as you are, to follow him. You must respond with limitless generosity.

For Reflection

Go through this exercise with the greatest possible realism, as a personal and authentic promise and response to Christ. You should approach it with the sense that it is critical to how you live the rest of your life. Whatever your state of life or personal situation, whatever plans God may have for you, something really hangs in the balance here. In doing this exercise, you walk in the footsteps of many others who have responded to the Lord's call and made a difference in the world.

More words of Jesus to reflect on:

"Do not think that I have come to bring peace on earth . . ." (Matthew 10:34-39).

"I will follow you wherever you go . . . " (Luke 9:57-62).

How to Contemplate the Life of Christ

What does it mean to struggle for the kingdom? Who are the enemies to be subjected? What means should we use? How do we live for God in Christ Jesus? We have already touched on these themes. In the following exercises, we will explore them more fully by considering various mysteries, or aspects, of the life of Christ.

The personal discovery and interiorization of spiritual truths is the work of the Holy Spirit in each soul. Only he can make us understand—in its deepest sense and in its implications for our own life and personal vocation—what Christ taught by his words, actions, works, and behavior. Only the Holy Spirit can form in our being the image of Christ Jesus, which must mature there. Truly, the Spirit is the soul of our life in Christ.

In complete openness to the action of the Spirit, then, we will now begin to pray by contemplating the mysteries and various events of the life of Christ. Each one of his gestures, words, and attitudes holds a call. As we follow, we can act like Christ in the conquest of his kingdom and submission of his enemies. The Holy Spirit will help us hear these invitations, if we listen for his voice. In his light, through his inspirations and stirrings, we will adopt the right attitude toward these invitations and discover what they mean. Now more than ever is the time to cultivate a disposition of spiritual peace, simplicity, humility, docility, and silent attention to the Spirit.

Here is the general approach we will take for these exercises, in which we recall the mysteries of Christ's life, as narrated in the gospel:

- Through the usual *preparatory prayer*, we aim to purify our intention by fixing it exclusively on the service and praise of God. (The prayer is found on page 28 and is number 46 of the *Spiritual Exercises*.)

- We put aside our intellectual preoccupations and prejudices and open ourselves to the gospel with that supreme confidence which is born from faith in the Spirit. This Holy Spirit assists and has assisted his Church throughout all generations, without ever contradicting himself.

- With this attitude of trust, we use our imagination for the *composition of place*—that is, to envision the place in which each particular mystery, or event, unfolds.

- In each mystery, we ask for the grace of the interior knowledge of Christ which he wants to bring to life in a uniquely personal way—"for me," so that we may love and follow him more completely.

- In some contemplations, we will also "see" the persons who appear in the particular event—hearing what they say, observing what they do, trying to discern the inner attitudes that motivate them.

  We picture all this as if we ourselves were present and acting in the scene which is unfolding. In faith, we feel and live out the mystery we contemplate. In this way, we confirm for ourselves that the power with which Christ lived out these very same mysteries for the salvation and sanctification of all mankind transcends history, reaching even to our generation. The contemplative imagination is the framework that reveals this mystery, provided we open ourselves to the light of the Spirit. Then we will feel his inspirations, which will move us to faith, hope, and love.

- Next, we must move from imagination to daily-life application. In this way, the incarnation continues in our day. Through the continuous action of the Holy Spirit, the mystery of Christ comes to birth in each soul. While this does not happen through a simple intention of our will, we cooperate by following Christ with fidelity and docility to the Spirit which has been given us (Romans 5:5).

- Finally, we should remember, as we contemplate, that a prayer of petition is always appropriate. The Lord desires these prayers, which may be expressed in spontaneous conversations with him (*colloquies*), in formal prayers, gestures, or however else the Spirit leads.

  These are the attitudes and the overall process with which we will now begin to meditate on the mysteries of Christ's life. Through these contemplations, may you come to a more intimate knowledge of the Lord. May you enter into deeper friendship with him and come to love and follow him more closely as you work with him for the coming of his kingdom.

For Reflection

How well do I know the Holy Spirit? Do I seek his light and guidance? What can I do to get better acquainted with him and open myself to his work?

Take a few minutes to reflect on the following Scripture verse. Then, ask the Holy Spirit to be your "Counselor"—especially during the coming days, as you read and meditate on the sacred word which he inspired.

"But the Counselor, the Holy Spirit, whom the Father will send in my name, he will teach you all things, and bring to your remembrance all that I have said to you" (John 14:26).

Using Scripture as his reference point, St. Ignatius situates this contemplation in three different scenes with a colossal sweep of imaginative vision: the entire world inhabited by human beings, the royal throne of the three divine Persons, and the room of Our Lady in Nazareth.

Words of St. Ignatius

After the usual *preparatory prayer*, we begin with an overview of the subject for contemplation: *Here it is how the three Divine Persons gazed on the whole surface or circuit of the world, full of people; and how, seeing that they were all going down into hell, they decide in their eternity that the Second Person should become a human being, in order to save the human race. And thus, when the fullness of time had come, they sent the angel St. Gabriel to Our Lady.* Then, St. Ignatius directs us to imagine two scenes: *the great extent of the circuit of the world, with peoples so many and so diverse; and then . . . in particular the house and rooms of Our Lady, in the city of Nazareth in the province of Galilee.*

The special prayer request of this contemplation: *to ask for an interior knowledge of Our Lord, who became human for me, that I may love him more intensely and follow him more closely.*

St. Ignatius shows how to go through this meditation point by point:

Point One: I will see the various persons, some here, some there.

First, those on the face of the earth, so diverse in dress and behavior: some white and others black, some in peace and others at war, some weeping and others laughing, some healthy and others sick, some being born and others dying, and so forth.

Second, I will see and consider the three Divine Persons, seated, so to speak, on the royal throne of Their Divine Majesty. They are gazing on the whole face and circuit of the earth; and they see all the peoples in such great blindness, and how they are dying and going down to hell.

Third, I will see Our Lady and the angel greeting her. Then I will reflect on this to draw some profit from what I see.

Point Two: I will listen to what the persons on the face of the earth are saying; that is, how they speak with one another, swear and blaspheme, and so on. Likewise, I will hear what the Divine Persons are saying, that is, "Let us work the redemption of the human race," and so forth. Then I will listen to what the angel and Our Lady are saying. Afterwards I will reflect on this, to draw profit from their words.

Point Three: Here I will consider what the people on the face of the earth are doing: How they wound, kill, go to hell, and so on. Similarly, what the Divine Persons are doing, that is, bringing about the most holy Incarnation, and other such activities. Likewise, what the angel and Our Lady are doing, with the angel carrying out his office of ambassador and Our Lady humbling herself and giving thanks to the Divine Majesty. Then I will reflect on these matters, to draw some profit from each of them.

Colloquy

I will think over what I ought to say to the Three Divine Persons, or to the eternal Word made flesh, or to our Mother and Lady. I will beg favors according to what I perceive in my heart, that I may better follow and imitate Our Lord, who in this way has recently become a human being. End with an Our Father.

(Spiritual Exercises, 101-104, 106-109)

For Reflection

Use all or some of the following Scripture passages as a help in grounding your meditation:

Luke 1:26-38—the Annunciation

John 1:1-18—the Word becomes flesh

Romans 1:18-32—the perverse foolishness of the world's rejecting God

Hebrews 10:5-7—"I have come to do your will"

John 3:16—the reason for the gift.

Commentary

Following the intention of St. Ignatius, I will try to see, hear, and observe the three scenes of this mystery as if I were present:

The World. The divine gaze sweeps over the world, which I must contemplate from a global perspective, as it is today. It is so diverse in so many ways—in its races, attitudes, living conditions, languages, customs. Some people are laughing, others are crying; some are being born, others dying; some are healthy, others sick. Some people are full, while others are so hungry they have become mere skeletons. Some defend life, but others kill it even before it is born. There are people at peace and others at war, people who love and others who hate.

This is the unhappy state of the world which has not yet received the grace of Christ. I should realize that it is my world, too, the sphere of my existence. I myself am immersed in this sinful confusion which Christ desires to illuminate and save.

Conversation in Heaven. I will contemplate the Father, Son, and Holy Spirit as they direct their gaze on earth's turmoil. From the heavens, the Most Holy Trinity looks upon these men and women who argue among themselves and run around blindly in the dark, so far from the dignity for which God destined them from the beginning of creation. Of course, there is no way to grasp the full reality of this scene in heaven! Who can penetrate the mind of God?

As you think about the Trinity, concentrate your spirit with the greatest possible reverence. Adore profoundly the divine decision on which our salvation depends. Through it, the Father will manifest his kindness and saving love to all humanity. His divine Son will more than make amends for our sins by becoming flesh and dying for us. He will also fill us with his Spirit and so enable us to lead lives worthy of God's sons and daughters.

With the deepest, most reverent gratitude, contemplate this initiative of the Father, the offering of the Son, the participation of the love of the Holy Spirit. This is the moment from which flows all our hope. St. Ignatius summarizes it in one sentence of imaginative dialogue: *Let us work the redemption of the human race* (*Spiritual Exercises*, 107). The Letter to the Hebrews presents Christ's loving acceptance of this mission. *Since animal sacrifices, offerings, and holocausts cannot make up for sin, here I am, Father, to do your will* (Hebrews 10:8-9). Notice that the cross is involved from the very beginning: "And by that will we have been sanctified through the offering of the body of Jesus Christ once for all" (10:10).

With Mary in Nazareth. But in our world of shadows and sin, God himself has prepared one pure heart to be the dwelling place of his Son. In this little town in Galilee called Nazareth lives a purity so exquisitely transparent that God's eternal Word will manifest himself there in the flesh, as a little child. This is a purity which finds full fruitfulness by its faith in the divine word: "And blessed is she who believed that there would be a fulfillment of what was spoken to her from the Lord" (Luke 1:45).

Contemplate the small house of Mary, half enclosed in the rock of the mountainside. It is just one among many in the little village of Nazareth. No one expects anything important to come from here. At this moment in history, Nazareth is practically unknown, and Palestine is an insignificant region under the yoke of the Roman Empire. Mary is a young girl with no worldly prestige. In her own town, people will express surprise that Jesus is her son: "Where did this man get this wisdom and these mighty works? Is not this the carpenter's son? Is not his mother called Mary?" (Matthew 13:54-55).

Mary is unnoticed in the eyes of the world, and she herself is aware of her littleness and total indebtedness to the Lord. But God has set his gaze on her. In her humility and initial embarrassment, Mary does not understand what the messenger of God means by his words: "Hail, full of grace, the Lord is with you" (Luke 1:28).

Read the entire dialogue in Luke 1:26-38, carefully noting Mary's words and reactions. Linger wherever you receive God's light or experience his consoling touch in your soul. Try to grasp the meaning of God's invitation to share the sublime adventure of this divine loving intimacy with an undivided heart.

Through Mary's intercession, let us ask for purity and for the graces of virginity for the sake of the kingdom, in a world that needs them so much. Only through an esteem for purity can so many enemies of the kingdom be overcome. May we know how to discover for ourselves Mary's total openness to divine grace. In her response there is not a single moment of withdrawal into herself. Once her question about how God's plan will unfold is resolved, her response is: "Behold I am the handmaid of the Lord; let it be to me according to your word" (Luke 1:38). And she, a virgin, becomes the mother of God and of all who will be one with Christ.

Let us contemplate, behind Mary's words, the genuflection of her heart. Her offering echoes that of the eternal Son. Mary can sense difficulties ahead: suspicion, possible repudiation, sorrows. But in her eyes, all that is important is to serve her Lord and obey his word.

Reflect on Mary the Virgin, in whom divinity desired to dwell. Her qualities point out the ways by which God's kingdom is penetrating this world and highlight the values esteemed in that kingdom. By her humble love, Mary helps us to appreciate what the Word of God did for us in his incarnation: "When you became man to set us free you did not spurn the Virgin's womb," the Church says in that great hymn of praise, the *Te Deum*.

Jesus begins his earthly life by being received into Mary's womb. Everything else will unfold from here: his road toward death, his humbling, his self-abasement and self-emptying. As a result, the emptiness of our human existence—with all its limitations, narrowness, and confines—is now filled with his truth, life, light, and powerful energy. Looking at Jesus, we understand that true glory is found in humility, true riches in giving up riches, true life in death. This is the scandal and the wisdom of the cross—the royal throne established on the place of execution.

For Reflection

Following your inclinations, express your thoughts about this exercise to the Blessed Virgin, to Jesus, to the Holy Spirit, or to the Father. In your conversation, ask for a loving knowledge of Jesus and for the ability to imitate his actions, attitudes, and preferences so as to better follow him in conquering the enemies of his kingdom. If you feel moved toward something or enlightened about some decision for your life, you can note that here.

More on Contemplating the Life of Christ

Here are a few more suggestions for getting the most out of your contemplation of scenes from the infancy and later life of Jesus Christ.

Put yourself in the picture. As you did in the last exercise, try to put yourself into the scenes you are contemplating. See what the people in them are doing; listen to what they are saying. But don't be just a spectator! It is essential that you enter in. Let yourself be absorbed by the mystery and open to its action, following the light and movement of the Spirit of God.

Be open to the Holy Spirit. With each mystery, the Spirit will impress certain points on you—either internal attitudes or external decisions. However, you must learn to be attentive to the Spirit's mysterious activity in you and remain open to it. "Truly, I say to you, unless you turn and become like children, you will never enter the kingdom of heaven" (Matthew 18:3).

Take your time. It is important that you take the time to rest serenely with these contemplations of Christ's life. This allows for spontaneous opportunities when the Holy Spirit can impress on you the features corresponding to the image of Christ, which he desires to form in you. Cooperate with this work by cultivating silence, peace, and relaxed attentiveness.

Less may be more. Rather than trying to consider many mysteries or reflections about them, it is better to spend sufficient time on each one you have selected. You might even repeat or review something that you have contemplated before. This has an advantage. Once the field has been cleared and the novelty of the initial encounter has passed, the soul enters with more spontaneity and without haste into the mystery. It is more open to the new levels where the Holy Spirit wants to lead it.

A new way of sensing. By spending sufficient time with a gospel scene, you will learn to explore it not only by imaginatively using your physical senses, such as seeing and hearing, but also what St. Ignatius suggests, your "spiritual" senses. For example, you can "inhale" the delicate odor of the evangelical virtues and "taste" the attractiveness of the interior attitudes of many gospel figures and the sweetness flowing from intimate friendship with Jesus. This is an experience which can carry over into your daily life, through moments of quiet prayer.

The Birth of Jesus

Words of St. Ignatius

Begin with the usual *preparatory prayer*, and then consider the story you are about to contemplate. *Recall how Our Lady, pregnant almost nine months and, as we may piously meditate, seated on an ass, together with Joseph and a servant girl leading an ox, set forth from Nazareth to go to Bethlehem and pay the tribute which Caesar had imposed on all those lands.*

Imagine the place. See *the road from Nazareth to Bethlehem. Consider its length and breadth, whether it is level or winds through valleys and hills. Similarly, look at the place or cave of the Nativity: How big is it, or small? How low or high? And how is it furnished?*

Ask for the same grace as in the last exercise: *an interior knowledge of Our Lord, who became human for me, that I may love him more intensely and follow him more closely.*

More specifically, St. Ignatius proposes these points for reflection:

Point One: I will *see the persons; that is, to see Our Lady, Joseph, the maidservant, and the infant Jesus after his birth. I will make myself a poor, little, and unworthy slave, gazing at them, contemplating them, and serving them in their needs, just as if I were there, with all possible respect and reverence. Then I will reflect upon myself to draw some profit.*

Point Two: I will observe, consider, and contemplate what they are saying. Then, reflecting upon myself, I will draw some profit.

Point Three: I will *behold and consider what they are doing; for example, journeying and toiling, in order that the Lord may be born in greatest poverty; and that after so many hardships of hunger, thirst, heat, cold, injuries, and insults, he may die on the cross! And all this for me! Then I will reflect and draw some spiritual profit.*

Conclude with a colloquy, as in the preceding contemplation, and with an Our Father.

(Spiritual Exercises, 110-117)

For Reflection

Make sure to read and reflect on Luke 2:1-20 as your starting point for this contemplation. As an aid to putting yourself in the scene, you might:

- note any words or phrases that strike you, and use those to spur your imagination

- choose a character, and move through the event from that person's perspective.

Commentary

In order to contemplate the mystery of the birth of Jesus, we will accompany Mary and Joseph, following the sequence of the gospel narrative.

We begin *in Nazareth*, when official notice confirms the edict of Caesar Augustus ordering a census of the entire world; each person is to be registered in the city of his family's origins. How did people react as word of the edict spread? There must have been criticisms, protests, and insubordination. Imagine and compare these reactions with the docile, serene, diligent, and confident responses of Mary and Joseph.

Assist them as they prepare for the journey, and then accompany these two custodians of the divine treasure of salvation *along the road to Bethlehem*. Contemplate their every step and encounter along the way. Imagine their modesty, composure, and faith in the mystery whose bearers they feel themselves to be during the hardships of the journey. Mary is the true Ark of the Covenant.

See how *in Bethlehem*, Joseph and Mary find all possibilities for shelter closed to them, even the inn. Observe their measured reactions, which reflect their confidence in the providence of the Father, who knows how to guide all things for the good of his chosen ones. As their example demonstrates, we should learn to detect the will of God through the events of our lives. God's mysterious plans will come to pass despite the obvious difficulties. Mary and Joseph put no obstacles in the way. Like the thin reed on the river bank that bends to the slightest breeze, they know how to submit to the divine will. Christ will appear in the world in the straw of a manger, choosing to begin the new era of the Spirit in humility and poverty. In all generations, contemplative eyes will discover him there and be absorbed with joy and marveling adoration.

Think about this: Only one person has ever been able to choose where and how to be born—Jesus, the Son of God, who existed before coming into this world. Amazingly, he chose to experience not only the total dependence with which all human life begins, but also exterior deprivation and abandonment by all except Mary and Joseph. Imagine these sufferings of the Holy Family—encamped on the outskirts of the town, without a house, without furniture, without human help, their provisions for the journey exhausted. How different God's plans, projects, and preferences are from those of human beings!

Jesus did not have himself announced with thundering publicity or make his appearance in the rich districts of Jerusalem. He preferred to present himself *without honors* or demands and to make himself known in modest simplicity: "You will find a babe wrapped in swaddling cloths and lying in a manger" (Luke 2:12).

Let us take in this peaceful and gentle environment and allow ourselves to be moved by it. May the Holy Spirit help us to become attracted by the spiritual radiance of these *poor of Yahweh* who had been prepared to receive the good news: his humble servant, the Virgin Mary; Joseph, the just man who walked in the law of the Lord; the shepherds, those night workers whose hearts were obedient, kind, and open to the messages from above. They were able to discover and adore Jesus, to rejoice immensely in his presence, and to communicate their joy to others.

In the Nativity, greed, superficiality, and pride—those enemies of the kingdom—receive the divine death blow. Jesus lies in the manger, and those who have put all their trust in Yahweh come to him bearing the gifts of their simple, humble hearts.

For Reflection

Allow the Spirit to impress the grace of this mystery on you by reflecting on some contrasts: the importance of Christ's mission and his apparently insignificant entrance into the world . . . what God values and what the world values . . . God's wisdom and human wisdom. . . . If time allows, read what St. Paul wrote to the members of the church in Corinth, who were apparently lacking in worldly prestige: 1 Corinthians 1:23-31.

If you wish to continue your contemplation on the birth of Jesus, you can elaborate on these points about the shepherds, from St. Ignatius:

Point One: The birth of Christ our Lord is made known to the shepherds by an angel: "I bring you good news of great joy, for this day is born to you the Savior of the world."

Point Two: The shepherds go to Bethlehem: "They came with haste; and they found Mary and Joseph and the Infant lying in the manger."

Point Three: "The shepherds returned, glorifying and praising God."

(Spiritual Exercises, 265)

Persons who are already willing to serve God in all things despite what the world may say about them and despite future persecutions or difficulties will no longer be tempted by Satan with carnal pleasures or glories. He sees that they would reject even the slightest direct suggestion of sinning. They will experience the diabolical attack through something that appears to be a good for the glory of God—something attractive, such as a temporal or spiritual benefit for themselves or their neighbor. Satan will hide his evil intentions, while exposing these persons to dangers they cannot withstand and disturbing them with proposals contrary to God's will for them. Little by little, they come to hate the good or are led off the right path or do something less good than what they had resolved to do previously.

For persons of this type, St. Ignatius has proposed norms of spiritual discernment which are more subtle and difficult to apply than those we examined during the first week of the *Exercises* (see page 53). Here is a summary of some of these rules. Be advised, though, that it is best to apply them with the aid of a spiritual director.

Words of St. Ignatius

The first criterion for judging is this: In fervent souls, *it is characteristic of God and his angels . . . to give genuine happiness and spiritual joy, and thereby to banish any sadness and turmoil induced by the enemy.*

In contrast, *it is characteristic of the enemy to fight against this happiness and spiritual consolation, by using specious reasonings, subtleties, and persistent deceits.*

The second and third criteria: *Only God our Lord can give the soul consolation without a preceding cause.* Here, St. Ignatius is referring to a spiritual joy or refreshment that has not originated in or been stimulated by any previous perception, knowledge, or sentiment. The situation is not so clear when a consolation is stimulated by a "preceding cause," such as a thought arising out of meditation. Either the "good angel" or the "evil angel" may be the cause: the good spirit for the progress of the soul, the evil spirit for the contrary purpose.

The fourth criterion: *The evil angel, who takes on the appearance of an angel of light,* enters by first *going along the same way as the devout soul,* but later exits by his own way. That is, he arrives with *good and holy thoughts attractive to such an upright soul,* but gradually entices it over to his own evil intentions.

The fifth criterion: *We should pay close attention to the whole train of our thoughts. If the beginning, middle, and end are all good and tending toward what is wholly good, it is a sign of the good angel. But if the train of the thoughts . . . ends up in something evil or diverting, or in something less good that what the soul was originally proposing to do; or further, if it weakens, disquiets, or disturbs the soul by robbing it of the peace, tranquility, and quiet which it enjoyed earlier, all this is a clear sign that this is coming from the evil spirit, the enemy of our progress and eternal salvation. . . .*

The eighth criterion: Even when the consolation has no "preceding cause," when it comes from God and leads to good, *the spiritual person ought to examine that experience with great vigilance and attention. One should distinguish the time when the consolation itself was present from the time after it*—immediately after it, especially. Favored by these gifts and full of fervor, we might add something of our own concepts or be influenced by other spirits which would not be coming immediately from God. Any convictions or plans we might form as a result would need to be carefully examined before being fully accepted or put into effect.

(See Spiritual Exercises, 328-336)

Once again, these norms are best applied with the aid of a spiritual director.

The following meditation "points" are among the sketches and suggestions that St. Ignatius provided for additional contemplations of the life of the Lord. It would be best to use them according to the method you have already followed in the preceding exercises.

Begin with the usual *preparatory prayer*.

Recall the *history* or overview of the mystery or event you are about to contemplate.

In the *composition of place*, imagine the scene and see yourself as present in it.

Ask for the special graces you want to receive through this contemplation.

Consider the *points for contemplation*.

In the *colloquy*, speak to Jesus, the Father, the Holy Spirit, or Mary about your reflections and offer yourself for God's service once again.

End with an Our Father, Soul of Christ, or Hail Mary.

Luke 2:22-38

The Presentation of Jesus in the Temple and the Purification of Our Lady

Words of St. Ignatius

Point One: They carry the infant Jesus to the temple, to present him to the Lord as the first-born son, and they offer for him "a pair of turtledoves and two young pigeons."

Point Two: Simeon, coming to the temple, "took him into his arms" and said: "Now you dismiss your servant, O Lord, in peace."

Point Three: Afterwards Anna, "coming in, confessed to the Lord and spoke of him to all who looked for the redemption of Israel."

(Spiritual Exercises, 268)

Commentary

The Holy Family is not ashamed of being poor and presenting themselves at the temple as poor folk. They come bringing the gifts proper to the poor: a pair of turtledoves or pigeons.

Simeon, who was waiting for the redemption of Israel, met them in the temple. He was in intimate contact with the Holy Spirit—attentive to his movements, listening for his deep and personal communications. How Simeon's attention must have increased suddenly when the Holy Family came into view! Notice the natural harmony that draws together souls in which the same divine Spirit dwells and is at work.

The inspired elder holds the mystery of Jesus before the eyes of Joseph and Mary, eliciting their wonder. A sign of contradiction, ruin and resurrection, a sword that will pierce the mother's heart. . . . Even in the joy of Christ's beginnings, trials are announced. Mary's sorrow is integrated in the plan of redemption. From now on, Mary cannot think of herself apart from the mystery of her divine son.

Contemplate the virtues of the people in the scene. Silence and modesty are exhibited by Mary and Joseph, who are faithful followers and lovers of God's law.

Simeon is the "just and devout" man. Anna is a model of pious perseverance in prayer and penance. In the eyes of the world, none of these people is doing anything worthy of esteem, yet it is they who grasp the great joy of the good news and communicate it to a waiting humanity.

With Jesus' entrance into the temple, the temple becomes the Church. Jesus' presence brings salvation for all the nations. In Jesus, all believers are united as God's new people.

For Reflection

Mary was keenly aware that the poor hold a privileged place before God. We may pray her song of praise, the *Magnificat*, and ask for the grace to see this, too: Luke 1:46-55.

Matthew 2:13-23

The Flight into Egypt and the Return

Use the method of prayer described on pages 83 and 91 to meditate on these mysteries of Christ's life.

Words of St. Ignatius

Point One: Herod wanted to kill the infant Jesus and therefore slew the Innocents. But before their death an angel warned Joseph to flee into Egypt: "Arise, and take the child and his mother, and flee into Egypt."

Point Two: He arose by night, and departed for Egypt.

Point Three: He remained there until the death of Herod.

Point One: The angel tells Joseph to return to Israel: "Arise, and take the child and his mother, and go into the land of Israel."

Point Two: He arose and went into the land of Israel.

Point Three: Because Archelaus, son of Herod, was reigning in Judaea, he retired to Nazareth.

(Spiritual Exercises, 269-270)

For Reflection

There are good and bad behaviors in these scenes. Which ones do you feel drawn to reflect on for your life? The earnest obedience of Joseph? That of the Virgin Mary? Why?

What do you learn from observing them?

How does this relate to your finding the will of God for your own life?

What strikes you as you consider Christ's being subjected to wicked situations in his earthly life?

Luke 2:41-52

Jesus Remains in the Temple Without His Parents' Knowledge

Words of St. Ignatius

Point One: Christ our Lord at the age of twelve went up from Nazareth to Jerusalem.

Point Two: Christ our Lord remained in Jerusalem, and his parents did not know it.

Point Three: After three days, they found him seated among the doctors and conversing with them. When his parents asked him where he had been, he replied: "Did you not know that I ought to be concerned with my Father's business?"

(Spiritual Exercises, 272)

Commentary

The Son of God, he who is always and everywhere in the Father, is the adorer in spirit and in truth *par excellence*. He fulfills the law, participates in the religious and national ceremonies of his people, goes in pilgrimage to the temple of Jerusalem. Humility in the spiritual life makes it possible for him to accept the Mosaic law and legitimate norms of worship.

Enter into the feeling with which Jesus participates in the ceremonies, sings the psalms, lives the deep significance of the celebration and each of the symbols of the Passover. He is the Lamb of God, who takes away the sin of the world.

Imagine how he turns to his Father in prayer: "In the days of his flesh, Jesus offered up prayers and supplications . . . and he was heard because of his reverent submission" (Hebrews 5:7).

Contemplate the mystery of Jesus' staying behind in Jerusalem without telling his parents. They are pained, and he is concerned about them. But note that Jesus has not really explained his conduct, and Mary and Joseph do not understand his reply.

Besides the normal and ordinary basics laid down by God in the commandments, there is this most personal call that comes from above. Jesus must follow this call, even when it causes sorrow for the moment and entails difficulties: misunderstanding, stepping out into the unknown, sacrifice, and risk.

Notice that Jesus is aware of his sonship and his work with respect to the Father. In time, Mary, too, will become aware of this supernatural distance, which Jesus will often recall.

Jesus said to Mary: "O woman, what have you to do with me? My hour has not yet come." But he also said: "My mother and my brothers are those who hear the word of God and do it" (John 2:4; Luke 8:21).

When a woman in the crowd raised her voice and said to him, "Blessed is the womb that bore you, and the breasts that you sucked!", he said, "Blessed rather are those who hear the word of God and keep it!" (Luke 11:27-28).

What is Mary's attitude before the words of her son, which she does not understand? She preserves them in her heart as a precious treasure, in order to meditate on them. The Spirit will bring her to understand their profound meaning and what they will require of her.

For Reflection

Jesus' example shows us that there are vocations which are, beyond a certain point, incompatible with normal home life. But for all followers of Jesus, there is some type of leaving behind, some expression of willingness to put God's will above everything else.

Reflect on these themes using the following passages:

"And every one who has left houses or brothers or sisters or father or mother or children or lands, for my name's sake, will receive a hundredfold, and inherit eternal life" (Matthew 19:29).

"He who loves father or mother more than me is not worthy of me; and he who loves son or daughter more than me is not worthy of me; and he who does not take his cross and follow me is not worthy of me. He who finds his life will lose it, and he who loses his life for my sake will find it" (Matthew 10:37-39).

____

____

____

____

____

____

____

____

____

____

____

____

____

____

____

Luke 2:40,51-52; Matthew 13:54-55

The Hidden Life of Nazareth

Words of St. Ignatius

Point One: He was obedient to his parents, "and Jesus advanced in wisdom, and age, and grace."

Point Two: It seems that he practiced the trade of carpenter, as St. Mark seems to indicate [6:3]: "Is not this, surely, the carpenter?"

(Spiritual Exercises, 271)

Commentary

Invisible to human eyes. Our Lord's "hidden life" in Nazareth is the most splendid renunciation of a life of importance in the eyes of the world. The only thing extraordinary in these years is their religious value, which is visible only to the gaze of God. The source of perseverance and strength is hidden in what is invisible.

But how was it possible for the most excellent human "personality" that has ever existed to hide itself? Jesus' merits go virtually unnoticed by others for thirty years. "Where did this man get this wisdom and these mighty works?" the people of Nazareth will ask (Matthew 13:54). For them, Jesus is the son of a common worker, like so many others. They know his parents.

To picture Jesus among his contemporaries is to consider the mystery of Christian humility. He shares the ordinary life of all the rest, yet he is so different. They do not notice him any more than they notice the air that they breathe.

Hidden life. Consider Jesus' hidden life with the Father in the light of this passage:

> But when you give alms, do not let your left hand know what your right hand is doing, so that your alms may be in secret; and your Father who sees in secret will reward you. . . . When you pray, go into your room and shut the door and pray to your Father who is in secret; and your Father who sees in secret will reward you.... When you fast, anoint your head and wash your face, that your fasting may not be seen by men but by your Father who is in secret; and your Father who sees in secret will reward you. (Matthew 6:3-4,6,17-18)

Family life. The Gospels do not give us a description of everyday life in the home at Nazareth, but we can well imagine that this is a family in which each member considers himself the least and at the service of the others. They are of one heart and one mind. Let us imaginatively listen in on their conversation. It does not put up barriers; it does not chill or sadden spirits. It elevates, unites, stretches, and opens horizons. Imagine, too, how Jesus, Mary, and Joseph help one another in their words and in their works and how they pray together, building up the bonds of true intimacy.

Jesus "was obedient to them" (Luke 2:51). Jesus is the Son of God, and however virtuous they were, Mary and Joseph were human beings. Even so, Jesus related to them as an obedient son. "For as by one man's disobedience many were made sinners, so by one man's obedience many will be made righteous" (Romans 5:19). We must not fear confronting the mystery of our Christian obedience.

God's wisdom. If we had been in charge of designing the Savior's life, how very differently we would have distributed his years on earth and his occupations. Instead of thirty years of hidden life and barely two or three as a public figure, wouldn't we have chosen the complete reverse? This is a sign that we will have to correct many of our impressions about what contributes to the establishment of the kingdom of God. God's ways of acting do not coincide with many of our ideas about human progress.

Taking on God's criteria for progress requires a sort of "Copernican revolution" in our way of thinking. It involves an inclination toward:

- obscurity, instead of anxieties to do something to distinguish ourselves;
- a sense of calm, which will cure our worries about rushing ahead and getting somewhere as soon as possible;
- the monotony of the same work, versus our search for change;
- composure and seclusion, to counter our restless urges to go out and see the world;
- depth, opposed to our superficiality;
- God's serious work, in contrast with our tendency toward laziness.

Nazareth is the school of anchoring ourselves in the will of God: "How much better is one single act of perfect love by the Church than all the apostolates of the world" (St. John of the Cross, *The Spiritual Canticle*, XXIX,2). This pure love is the union of my will with God's.

For Reflection

Ask the Holy Spirit to help you identify areas where you need a change of mind so that you can better appreciate the slow, hidden ways in which God works.

Contemplating the life of Christ should create in us attitudes that correspond to his. Especially, we should be growing in desire to work with him in the establishment of his kingdom, according to our generous offering of self. These attitudes include dispositions of the soul, virtuous inclinations, and love of the virtues we find in Jesus.

But during the *Exercises*, we should also take a concrete look at our decisions. What choices does God want me to make so that my life will unfold according to his will for me? This is an especially relevant question if I am facing a choice about my state in life, or some other important decision. How does the Lord wish to use me for the service of his kingdom?

St. Ignatius uses the term "elections" to refer to this act of making choices and decisions in view of God's call and the circumstances of our lives. Only with the grace of God can such a venture be successful. But since we ourselves have been chosen by God, we know that he has definite plans for us (Ephesians 1:4). The "elections" are therefore a matter of recognizing and receiving what God has chosen. They are not decisions we arrive at only through our own reflection.

Because making decisions according to God's will means committing your life to a concrete journey, the process usually entails great difficulties and apprehension. At times you may feel that your understanding has become disturbed and covered with darkness. The will feels resistance or bewilderment and reacts by asserting itself with almost violent force. You may be bombarded by unruly emotions, as often happens. More than ever, this is the time to humbly ask God for serenity and perseverance!

Foreseeing such situations, St. Ignatius proposed several unique meditations designed to orient people who are in the immediate process of "elections" of one kind or another. In order to understand the exercises that follow, you must already have resolved not only to avoid all that is evil, but to embrace whatever is clearly better.

A Meditation on the Two Standards

In the spirit of the Letter to the Ephesians, St. Ignatius evokes the clash of good and evil and our part in the battle: "Put on the whole armor of God, that you may be able to stand against the wiles of the devil" (Ephesians 6:11). In this meditation, "standards" are both the banners or flags around which followers of leaders rally and also sets of norms and values.

Words of St. Ignatius

After the *preparatory prayer*, I will think about the "history" I am about to consider, namely, *how Christ calls and desires all persons to come under his standard, and how Lucifer in opposition calls them under his.*

The "composition of place": *Here it will be to imagine a great plain in the region of Jerusalem, where the supreme commander of the good people is Christ our Lord; then another plain in the region of Babylon, where the leader of the enemy is Lucifer.*

The grace to be sought in making this meditation: *insight into the deceits of the evil leader, and for help to guard myself against them; and further, for insight into the genuine life which the supreme and truthful commander sets forth, and grace to imitate him.*

The Standard of Satan

Point One: Imagine the leader of all the enemy in that great plain of Babylon. He is seated on a throne of fire and smoke, in aspect horrible and terrifying.

Point Two: Consider how he summons uncountable devils, disperses some to one city and others to another, and thus throughout the whole world, without missing any provinces, places, states, or individual persons.

Point Three: Consider the address he makes to them: How he admonishes them to set up snares and chains; how first they should tempt people to covet riches (as he usually does, at least in most cases) so that they may more easily come to vain honor from the world, and finally to surging pride. In this way, the first step is riches, the second is honor, and the third is pride; and from these three steps the enemy entices them to all the other vices.

The Standard of Christ

Similarly, in contrast, gaze in imagination on the supreme and true leader, who is Christ our Lord.

Point One: Consider how Christ our Lord takes his place in that great plain near Jerusalem, in an area which is lowly, beautiful, and attractive.

Point Two: Consider how the Lord of all the world chooses so many persons, apostles, disciples, and the like. He sends them throughout the whole world, to spread his doctrine among people of every state and condition.

Point Three: Consider the address which Christ our Lord makes to all his servants and friends whom he is sending on this expedition. He recommends that they endeavor to aid all persons, by attracting them, first, to the most perfect spiritual poverty, and also, if the Divine Majesty should be served and should wish to choose them for it, even to no less a degree of actual poverty; and second, by attracting them to a desire of reproaches and contempt, since from these results humility.

In this way there will be three steps: the first, poverty in opposition to riches; the second, reproaches or contempt in opposition to honor from the world; and the third, humility in opposition to pride. Then from these three steps they should induce people to all the other virtues.

A Colloquy should be made with Our Lady. I beg her to obtain for me grace from her Son and Lord that I may be received under his standard; and first, in the most perfect spiritual poverty; and also, if his Divine Majesty should be served and if he should wish to choose me for it, to no less a degree of actual poverty; and second, in bearing reproaches and injuries, that through them I may imitate him more, if only I can do this without sin on anyone's part and without displeasure to the Divine Majesty. Then I will say a Hail Mary.

A Second Colloquy. It will be to ask the same grace from the Son, that he may obtain it for me from the Father. Then I will say the Soul of Christ.

A Third Colloquy will be to ask the same grace from the Father, that he may grant it to me. Then I will say an Our Father.

(Spiritual Exercises, 136-147)

For Reflection

Imagine the scene in the two opposing camps, and note some features of each.

What differences between the two opposing camps do you find most striking?

Why do you think Satan tells his troops to focus on the specific temptations of riches, honor, and pride?

Commentary

The purpose of this meditation is to shed light on both the deceits of the enemy and the true life taught by Christ and to obtain the grace to avoid Satan's way and follow Christ's. The two standards correspond to two armies with their respective leaders. Christ has pitched camp near Jerusalem and Satan near Babylon—two cities with great symbolic meaning in the Christian tradition. The meditation is a way of representing what revelation teaches about the spiritual struggle that has gone on since the beginning of history: The prince of shadows wants humanity to be lost, and Christ wants to save it in freedom. The decisive battle begins and ends in the heart of each one of us. Through our individual decisions, we place ourselves under one banner or the other, either advancing the cause of Christ or fighting more or less consciously for Satan's camp.

In the Camp of Babylon. Satan, the "father of lies," aims to deceive and presents himself with an imposing and overwhelming majesty that is not rightfully his. St. Ignatius directs us to imagine him *seated on a throne of fire and smoke, in aspect horrible and terrifying.* "Keep alert," St. Peter cautions, for this enemy is "like a roaring lion. . . looking for someone to devour" (1 Peter 5:8). The warning is always relevant, for there is no situation in this world where we are off limits to the evil spirits under the tempter's command. They threaten us all, so we must humbly ask God to free us from every binding snare.

St. Ignatius proposes an illuminating synthesis of the enemy's tactics which can help us detect and defeat them. He points out that the enemy's objective is to bring us to pride, because the proud person can be dragged toward any other vice. Normally, this is a two-step procedure.

First, by ensnaring the soul with the ambition for some kind of riches, Satan stirs up the deep-seated attitude of possessiveness, the desire to own things on which to rely, rest, relax, and find consolation. The second step is the desire to be esteemed for these possessions. People who fall for this tactic become ambitious for honors and want to be seen as important. Anxious to maintain their position at all costs, they begin to look at others as rivals, not as brothers and sisters, and eventually identify themselves with their possessions. They become arrogant and presumptuous, self-made individuals. Closed in on themselves and viewing themselves as the center of the universe, they reject correction and refuse the light that would reveal their defects. Instead, they seek the glory that comes from other people, even when it is based on lies and injustice. Such people have fallen into darkness and are ready for any sin.

The desire to possess and to be esteemed over others —these are the roots of fallen humanity's radical separation from God. This is the spirit that St. Augustine identified as characterizing the city of Babylon: "the love of self, even to the contempt of God." Let us accept the light to discover the strands of this diabolical net before they become enslaving chains that are almost impossible to break.

For Reflection

Use some of these Scripture passages in your meditation on "the camp of Babylon."

"Finally, be strong in the Lord and in the strength of his power. Put on the whole armor of God, so that you may be able to stand against the wiles of the devil. For our struggle is not against enemies of blood and flesh. . . " (Ephesians 6:10-17).

"Discipline yourselves; keep alert. Like a roaring lion your adversary the devil prowls around, looking for someone to devour. . . " (1 Peter 5:8-9).

"And do not bring us to the time of trial, but rescue us from the evil one" (Matthew 6:13).

"Stay awake and pray that you may not come into the time of trial; the spirit indeed is willing, but the flesh is weak" (Matthew 26:41).

"Keep me from the trap that they have laid for me, and from the snares of evildoers" (Psalm 141:9).

"How can you believe when you accept glory from one another and do not seek the glory that comes from the one who alone is God?" (John 5:44).

"Those who want to be rich fall into temptation and are trapped by many senseless and harmful desires that plunge people into ruin and destruction. . . " (1 Timothy 6:7-11).

Commentary

In the Camp of Jerusalem. Here the environment is peaceful and serene. Jesus is humble, simple, amiable, and wants everyone to receive the saving knowledge of the truth. His messengers are people whom he has made his friends, and he sends them out to the ends of the earth so that his message may reach every type and group of person.

The strategy of Jesus is totally contrary to that of Satan. He tells his friends and servants to help others become generously detached until they arrive at *the highest spiritual poverty*. Jesus calls all his followers to love poverty. Some he calls to actually leave their possessions in order to follow him more closely, with greater freedom and dedication. This breaks the ties to covetousness and sows an attitude of self-offering. Our spiritual poverty is genuine only if we are truly ready to give up actual or future possessions when we see that this is God's will.

Far from desiring riches, those who follow Christ must eventually arrive at the *desire for humiliations or contempt*. When persecuted, slandered, or otherwise harassed for the sake of Christ, they should be able to "rejoice and be glad at that time, for your reward is great in heaven" (Matthew 5:12). Just as Christ's disciples must love poverty and not fear having to do without in this world, they must also lose the fear of being despised and insulted. "If you were of the world, the world would love its own; but because you are not of the world, but I chose you out of the world, therefore the world hates you" (John 15:19). And even more than learning to put up with insults, we must rejoice to see our faults reproved and corrected, without excusing or denying them.

In this way, we will grow in *humility*. Seeing ourselves poor in goods, we will value ourselves more truly according to what we really are—not for what we own or what others say about us. Once established in humility, we are ready to receive all the other virtues as well, because "God opposes the proud, but gives grace to the humble" (James 4:6).

The enemy wants us to put our confidence and find our consolation in this world, in something other than our heavenly Father, so that our sense of independence will increase and lead us to usurp the place God should have in our lives. Christ, on the other hand, yearns to lead us to put all our confidence and find our entire consolation in God. "For where your treasure is, there will your heart be also" (Matthew 6:21). Only the detached and humble heart is able to love and pardon as Jesus taught us.

For Reflection

Have I reached the point where I can truly say that I desire poverty—or even appreciate its value? Is my approach to the good opinion of others consistent with the teaching and example of Christ? What stands in the way of my spiritual growth in these areas?

"Do not lay up for yourselves treasures on earth, where moth and rust consume and where thieves break in and steal, but lay up for yourselves treasures in heaven, where neither moth nor rust consumes and where thieves do not break in and steal. For where your treasure is, there will your heart be also" (Matthew 6:19-21).

Where is my treasure? Holy Spirit, give me light to explore, to understand myself—and to make whatever changes are necessary.

In my work, my family, and all my life circumstances, do I spread the love of poverty and set an example of suffering of injuries for Christ and true Christian humility?

Mary, my Mother, I want to take my place with you under the standard of your Son. Please help me to . . . *(continue according to your own needs)*.

Jesus, my Leader and Lord, here is my prayer to you:

Heavenly Father,

Three Classes of Persons

Words of St. Ignatius

Begin with the usual *preparatory prayer* and then consider the little story that St. Ignatius offers for reflection. It presents the situation of three individuals, each one typical of a certain type of person, who have suddenly inherited a large sum of money. All three become aware that the money has a hold on them and are disturbed by this. *Each desires to save his or her soul and to find God our Lord in peace, by discarding the burden and obstacle to this purpose which this attachment to the acquired money is found to be.*

Standing back from the story, turn to God by imagining yourself in the heavenly courts, *standing before God and all his saints* and wanting to *desire and know what will be more pleasing to the Divine Goodness. . . . Here I will ask for the grace to choose that which is more to the glory of the Divine Majesty and the salvation of my soul.*

Now consider the attitude that characterizes each of these three representative individuals:

The Person Typical of the First Class would like to get rid of this attachment to the acquired money, in order to find God in peace and be able to attain salvation. But this person does not take the means, even to the hour of death.

The Person Typical of the Second Class also desires to get rid of the attachment, but in such a way that she or he will keep the acquired money; and that thus God will come to where this person desires. No decision is made to dispose of the money in order to go where God is, even though that would be the better state for this individual.

The Person Typical of the Third Class desires to get rid of the attachment, but in such a way that there remains no inclination either to keep the acquired money or to dispose of it. Instead such a one desires to keep it or reject it solely according to what God our Lord will move one's will to choose, and also according to what the person himself or herself will judge to be better for the service and praise of the Divine Majesty.

In the meantime this person endeavors to take an attitude by which, as far as the affections are concerned, he or she is giving up everything. [In other words], one strives earnestly not to desire that money or anything else, except when one is motivated solely by the service of God our Lord; in such a way that the desire to be able to serve God our Lord better is what moves one to take or reject any object whatsoever.

(Spiritual Exercises, 149-157)

For Reflection

If today you won the lottery or unexpectedly inherited a fortune, do you think you would react more like person number one, number two, or number three? What evidence is there to support your answer?

Commentary

How easy it is to deceive ourselves! What does it cost us to say that we love poverty and insults when we lack nothing and are esteemed by others? We recognize our self-deception only when we experience poverty and need or insult and see ourselves retaliating to reclaim possessions and rights, esteem and compensation.

St. Ignatius designed this meditation to help us put our will to the test and see whether we are sincere. It aims to help us attain the disposition that is most effective for embracing whatever God may reveal about his will for our lives. St. Ignatius presents three types of persons who have suddenly become wealthy (and not through illegal means). They are basically well intentioned and want to find peace of mind and conscience. They know they cannot achieve this goal without giving up the attachment they feel for what they now own.

Each of these persons responds to the desire for inner peace in a different way, through different courses of action. You should meditate seriously on each response in order to choose for yourself the one which is the best and most effective—that is, the *most pleasing to his Divine Majesty and the benefit of one's soul.*

The Procrastinator. The first person is of two minds about his attraction to possessions: He wants to get free of it, but not badly enough. He delays making the decision and never confronts the problem resolutely. Perhaps he hopes that on his deathbed he will finally be spurred to resolve the issue! His worry about saving himself is genuine but does not bring him to act. Though he wants to serve God, he holds back in this critical area. He is fearful before the immensity of God, who wants to make himself present in our lives and lovingly direct our existence. He clings to himself, never achieving self-renunciation, never abandoning himself to God's love. He does not, in fact, resolve his problem.

The Controller. The second person also wants to overcome her attraction but refuses to entertain the possibility that the wealth must be given up. The only solution she will consider is to keep the money while not being "attached" to it. But what if this is impossible? What if detachment and peace of spirit require a willingness to part with one's possessions? This person will not consider that possibility and thus refuses to consider other alternatives. In the end, she does not submit to the will of God at all. She makes her choices—about how to use her riches and what to do with her life—and only afterwards determines how to serve God in the circumstances she has chosen. Instead of giving primary and unconditional acceptance to God's goals for her and then choosing the means that are best suited for achieving them, she acts as though God should accommodate himself to what she herself has chosen.

Persons of this type desire to serve God lovingly, but their wills do not succeed in renouncing themselves and their possessions in the ways that are necessary for all disciples of the Lord. Their attitudes and actions say, "Up to here, but no further," or, "On the one hand, yes, on the other hand, no." They relate to God as if he were their equal and place conditions as if he were their inferior. Expecting him to negotiate with their disordered desires and whims, they even bargain with him: "I'd like to get free of this attachment, but let me do what I want."

The Surrendered Person. The third type seeks with all their strength not to make any decision one way or another until their sole motive is to serve God our Lord. They will determine what to do with their money by lining up their own will with the will of God. In order to let God dispose of their goods, they fight against the interior attachment they feel by viewing their possessions as if they had already decided to give them up. This kind of person acts as if they had given a trustworthy person a blank check, with the instruction to return it only if it were clearly God's will.

For this person, then, God alone disposes. Detachment comes at a price, but because of it, the possibility of having to give up everything inspires no fear. What was such an obstacle for the first and second persons is actually a means of spiritual growth for this third one—renouncing everything in order to be a disciple of the Lord.

For Reflection

Go through this meditation slowly, reflectively, and as honestly as possible. Note whatever points strike you about the "three classes" and their relevance for your own life.

1. ___

2. ___

3.

As St. Ignatius advises, end this meditation as you did the last one, with a prayer to the Blessed Virgin, Jesus, and the Father. Ask to be allowed to serve under the standard of Christ. Ask for the grace to be detached and open to God's will—especially in areas where you face some important choice. Ask for the courage to choose what you least prefer, when this is God's will—whatever will most effectively realize the goal for which God created you.

Three Ways of Being Humble

"Far be it from me to glory except in the cross of our Lord Jesus Christ." (Galatians 6:14)

The aim of this exercise, like the meditations on the two standards and the three classes of persons, is to prepare for the "elections"—that is, for the upcoming exercise which focuses on making choices and decisions that further God's plan. Specifically, St. Ignatius intended that today's reflections on humility incline us, by God's grace, toward the imitation of Christ crucified. For love of us, Jesus was stripped of everything, covered with insults, thought to be crazy. What are we willing to sacrifice for love of him?

In the meditation on the two standards, humility was identified as the main goal to pursue in imitating and following Christ. Now it is time to gain a deeper understanding of this virtue so that we may become attracted to it to a higher degree.

St. Ignatius identified three ways of being humble (*Spiritual Exercises*, 165-168). These express the perfection of the Christian life. By means of them, you submit yourself more and more to the Lord until you find yourself totally at his disposal. You thus deepen your own *kenosis*, or self-emptying, casting aside the natural desire to be esteemed as someone important in order to attain to a deeper, more ardent humility which entails privation of worldly riches and honors. It is essential that you discover and reflect on the three ways of being humble so that you may fervently desire and request them.

The first way of being humble characterizes those who acknowledge the Lord and are so submitted to his will that nothing in the world can move them to decide to break any commandment that is binding under pain of mortal sin. Not for all the goods of the world or any hope of prosperity will they abandon their decision to submit to the Lord in all that is necessary for their eternal salvation. Neither can the threat of death or the fear of adversities cause them to vacillate before God's saving will. They are absolutely resolved not to let themselves be tricked into losing sight of their eternal destiny. Though they perhaps do not aspire to greater perfection and do let themselves be drawn aside by smaller matters sometimes, more or less on the spur of the moment, they generally *seek in all things to be obedient to the law of* God *our Lord.*

(Spiritual Exercises, 165)

For Reflection

Those who practice this first way of being humble live by the following watchwords. How might you incorporate them more into your mind for esteeming, requesting, and growing in love for this first way of being humble?

"Do not fear those who kill the body but cannot kill the soul; rather fear him who can destroy both soul and body in hell" (Matthew 10:28).

"And if your eye causes you to sin, pluck it out; it is better for you to enter the kingdom of God with one eye than with two eyes to be thrown into hell" (Mark 9:47).

The second way of being humble is more perfect, because those who live it are not more inclined to choose riches over poverty, honor over dishonor, or a long life over a short one, provided that each path brings equal glory to God our Lord. Once they see objectively that a particular means of perfection is best, therefore, they can choose it without any hesitation. This attitude of spirit makes them resolved to obey God's will in everything, even when it is a question of venial sin only. These lovers of humility have submitted themselves to the Creator and Lord to the point of desiring his will alone, right down to the slightest detail. Doing what pleases God in all things is more important to them than life, reputation, possessions, or anything else in this world.

Those who practice this second way of being humble have situated themselves in Christ. At least in intention, they can join in with Jesus' expression of humble obedience to the Father: "I always do what is pleasing to him" (John 8:29).

With the help of the Holy Spirit, ask yourself what you can do to advance in this way of being humble.

The third way of being humble is the most perfect: It includes the first and the second, while adding something more. It involves a greater renunciation of self and self-love in order to submit to the Lord more faithfully and surely. This way brings us as close as possible to embracing the will of God, as manifested in Christ. Again, provided that all options would equally further God's glory, we are not just indifferent or detached with regard to poverty, injuries, and everything that the world abhors: We become actually *inclined* toward them for love of Christ, who desired to endure all these things for love of us. With St. Ignatius, people who practice this third way of humility can say:

I desire and choose poverty with Christ poor rather than wealth; contempt with Christ laden with it rather than honors. Even further, I desire to be regarded as a useless fool for Christ, who before me was regarded as such, rather than as a wise or prudent person in this world.

(Spiritual Exercises, 167)

The reason for these preferences is to arrive at a closer resemblance to Christ. By taking on the concrete external circumstances that marked the Lord's life, we hope to take on his characteristics in our soul. This is the wisdom of the cross, which the world writes off as "foolishness." On the contrary, it is love—a love of Christ so audacious and strong that it leads us to embrace the cross. This love feels no need for other inducements.

Clearly, people who live this way are better prepared than others to endure things which they might otherwise find repugnant. Seeking to please God in all things, they are most able to make every concrete decision on the basis of giving greater glory to him. These humble people have emptied themselves of self, only to find themselves in Christ.

For Reflection

Many followers of the Lord have gone before us on this third way of humility and encourage us to do the same. What message do the following words of encouragement have for you?

"We must force ourselves to imitate the Lord in suffering greater offenses than the others, to be cheated more, and more despised; lest any plant of the devil be found among you, but rather that in all purity and moderation you may remain bodily and spiritually in Jesus Christ" (St. Ignatius of Antioch, *Letter to the Ephesians*, 10:3).

"I always would follow the road of suffering in order to follow our Lord Jesus Christ, even if there were no other gain." (St. Teresa of Avila, *The Interior Castle*, VI, 1,7).

St. Ignatius strongly recommends that in our three colloquies—to Mary, Jesus, and the Father—we ask *to be chosen for this third, a greater and better way of being humble*, for God's greater service and praise (*Spiritual Exercises*, 168).

Do you feel courageous enough to ask for this grace? To ask for the grace to even *desire* this grace?

This is the decision point of the *Spiritual Exercises* (169-189). Now is the moment to recognize the choices that God has put before you as his will, and to make and embrace them as a true Christian. Perhaps you are facing the major decision of choosing the state of life in which God our Lord wishes you to serve him. If this step is already behind you, perhaps you know of some life changes or reforms that the Lord wishes to see you introduce. Maybe some issues have surfaced as you have been going through these *Exercises*. Or you may need to decide among various alternatives in your particular situation: which proposal you should accept, which mission or job you should pursue, which opportunity you should act on.

Commentary

The children of God are those who allow themselves to be led by the Spirit of God (Romans 8:14). Once they recognize the specifics of what God wants, they choose his will and embrace his decision. Their intention is simple and pure: to desire only what leads to the greater service of the Lord and the salvation of their souls.

Clearly, St. Ignatius intended these elections to encompass only those things which are good or indifferent in themselves. In the case of anything already prohibited by God or the Church, or by some other legitimate authority, the choice has already been made: the will of God is manifest in the commandment or prohibition. The elections are a matter of finding and embracing God's will in matters where it has been unclear up till now but about which God our Lord now wishes to reveal his intention. God uses various means of leading us to understand his will for our individual lives.

Times when we cannot doubt. Sometimes he takes hold of the reins of our human will, drawing and moving us so that we do not doubt or wonder about what he wants. We simply know that God has put something in our spirit and that we are to follow it. (As those who have experienced this attraction can testify, it is neither stubbornness nor an obsession. To eliminate this possibility, however, the help of an experienced spiritual director is recommended.)

Perhaps you know people like this—men and women who are happy and fulfilled in their vocation and can look back and say they never had any doubts about how God was calling them to serve him. St. Ignatius presents St. Paul and St. Matthew as examples of people who experienced this clear revelation of God's will.

Gradually emerging patterns. Sometimes the Lord bring us to recognize his will little by little. Contact with Christ in prayer, deliberating about some decision, the memory of certain events, desiring to give ourselves more generously to Christ by identifying more closely with him—such experiences can awaken inner attractions or repulsions, consolations or desolations. Over time, as certain interior movements return, patterns may emerge and be discerned as the ordinary effects of the Holy Spirit: a peace that stabilizes us in the Lord, a spiritual joy that transcends human fear and anchors us in God, an increase in faith, hope and love. All of this may clarify the path by which the Lord wants to lead us here and now.

In this situation, two things are especially helpful: the review and evaluation of prayer after each day of the *Exercises* (see page 48) and some understanding of the "discernment of spirits" (see pages 53 and 97).

It is also good to consult a spiritual director. The director's role is to offer guidance, encouragement, and explanation; point out dangers along the path; confirm positive steps forward and indicate possibilities; confirm—or not confirm—the honesty and rightness of the discernment made by the person following the *Exercises*. The director is not there to make or impose any choice or decision, but must reverently refrain from interfering with God's work in a person's soul. The Creator must be allowed to accomplish what he intends.

Free and calm use of our natural faculties. When the Lord does not wish to manifest his will in other ways, he leaves it to us to make a choice through the calm and free use of our natural faculties. Here, St. Ignatius recommends several helps for reducing the risk of being overly subjective.

We should seek peace and objectivity by submitting our understanding and will to our Creator and Lord. If we can weigh alternatives according to their advantages and disadvantages rather than our inclinations and predispositions, we will be able to judge situations objectively, freely and calmly, and to choose rightly. Our intention must be pure, focused only on pleasing God and pursuing what is good for our soul. Having made our particular choice, we should bring it into the Lord's presence so that he may receive and confirm our offering.

Another way to seek objectivity in making decisions is to think about what I might advise another person in my situation—someone I do not know but want to see blessed with every good and perfection. Then I should follow this advice myself. Similarly, I could envision myself looking back at this decision from my deathbed or the moment of my judgment before God. What will I then wish I had chosen in this present situation? Which of these here-and-now choices will give me cause for joy at the end of my life?

And Remember . . . *Everyone ought to reflect that in all spiritual matters, the more one divests oneself of self-love, self-will, and self-interests, the more progress one will make* (*Spiritual Exercises*, 189).

Making these elections is not a matter of building a little cage of resolutions that keep us locked away from life's fearful responsibilities and risks. Our decisions regarding particular reforms in our life must always be open to what God's will may require of us through future events or new desires. "Unless the LORD builds the house, those who build it labor in vain" (Psalm 127:1).

The reformation of our lives is viewed as the trusting opening up of our soul to its Lord. With the simplicity of the dove and the prudence of a serpent, we seek to be vigilant in the Lord's service and to recognize his desires for us more clearly day by day. As best we can, we dispose ourselves to hear and obey whatever God wishes to manifest—and to keep on doing so throughout life!

For Reflection

Use this space to note thoughts that have especially struck you in this section.

An Outline of Review Points for Reforming My Life

Now and as you contemplate the public life of Christ in the next chapters, review before the Lord what he has shown you about his will for your life up to now. Investigate with him the new areas he desires to show you. You may find it useful to take notes and to use the following outline.

What change is God asking of me now in my prayer and sacramental life—daily, weekly, monthly?

Have I adopted any attitudes or habits that are not sinful in themselves but might jeopardize or damage my spiritual life in some way?

Has God shown me anything that I need to reform:

- in how I perform my duties at work?
- in the way I carry out my apostolate?
- in the witness of my life, both inside and outside my home?
- in my relationships with others: relatives, acquaintances, friends, superiors, and subordinates?

Where do I find the real obstacles to spiritual progress in my present circumstances? How should I focus my daily examination of conscience so as to face these specific struggles?

Toward what concrete attitudes, virtues, and decisions has the Lord directed me during these exercises?

Have I made my choice of a state of life with all faithfulness and sincerity before God? Will I approach the reform of my life in the same spirit?

Continue to assimilate the mysteries of the life of Christ, using the familiar method of prayer described on pages 83 and 91. Be especially attentive to the theme of your "elections," to what still needs to be clarified, and seek out the concrete ways in which you are called to contribute to the realization of God's kingdom.

Matthew 3:13-17; Mark 1:1-13; Luke 3: 1-22; John 1:19-34

The Baptism of Jesus

Words of St. Ignatius

Point One: Christ our Lord, after his farewell to his Blessed Mother, came from Nazareth to the river Jordan, where St. John the Baptist was.

Point Two: St. John baptized Christ our Lord; and when he sought to excuse himself because he thought himself unworthy to baptize him, Christ said to him: "Allow it now, for thus it is fitting for us to fulfill all righteousness."

Point Three: The Holy Spirit descended upon him, and the voice of the Father came from heaven and testified: "This is my beloved Son, in whom I am well pleased."

(Spiritual Exercises, 273)

Commentary

Jesus has arrived at the hour when he must leave his mother, home, and family life in Nazareth in order to dedicate himself exclusively to preaching the kingdom. Confident in the Father who sends him out, Jesus turns toward a future full of risk and adventure. His social status changes completely. From now on, he will be a rabbi, or traveling teacher, who goes about Israel accompanied by a group of disciples. He will work wonders and preach, responding to questions and teaching by word and example.

Make yourself present as Jesus takes leave of his mother. Try to enter into the generous self-offering of those two hearts.

In his journey to the Jordan, Jesus definitively turns his back on the tranquility of Nazareth. Recognize his absolute lack of material resources and the solitude of spirit with which he sets out to accomplish his mission. Converse with Jesus about all of this and listen to his interior dialogue with the Father, who is well pleased with him.

See John the Baptist, the precursor who prepares the way for the Messiah. Catch the spirit and atmosphere created by his preaching: "Bear fruits that befit repentance. . . . He who has two coats, let him share with him who has none; and he who has food, let him do likewise. . . . Rob no one by violence or by false accusation" (Luke 3:8,11,14). "After me comes a man who ranks before me, for he was before me. . . . whose sandal I am not worthy to untie. . . . He must increase, but I must decrease" (John 1:30,27; 3:30).

Contemplate Jesus with the wondering eyes of the Baptist: "I need to be baptized by you, and do you come to me?" (Matthew 3:14). See Jesus standing in line with those who are coming forward in repentance to receive the baptism of penance for the forgiveness of sins: "Behold, the Lamb of God, who takes away the sin of the world!" (John 1:29). Jesus clothes himself with the armor of humility as he begins his public struggle for the kingdom.

The Lamb of God has taken on our sins. "He was oppressed, and he was afflicted, yet he did not open his mouth; like a lamb that is led to the slaughter, and like a sheep that before its shearers is silent, so he did not open his mouth" (Isaiah 53:7). "He is the expiation for our sins, and not for ours only but also for the sins of the whole world," (1 John 2:2) "that the world might be saved through him" (John 3:17).

It is not the water which sanctifies Christ, but Christ who converts the water into an instrument of salvation:

> I myself did not know him; but he who sent me to baptize with water said to me, "He on whom you see the Spirit descend and remain, this is he who baptizes with the Holy Spirit." (John 1:33)

> But to all who received him, who believed in his name, he gave power to become children of God; who were born, not of blood nor of the will of the flesh nor of the will of man, but of God. (John 1:12-13)

> Jesus answered, "Truly, truly, I say to you, unless one is born of water and the Spirit, he cannot enter the kingdom of God." (John 3:5)

Let us hear the Father's solemn proclamation of Jesus as the Son of God and Messiah anointed by the Spirit. Christ, the humble one who has emptied himself of all, is glorified.

For Reflection

As you apply your imagination to Jesus' departure from Nazareth and his baptism, note whatever especially strikes you about the figures who play a part in these scenes:
Mary, Jesus, John the Baptist, God the Father.

What can you learn from Jesus' forward-looking move into his new life of public ministry? Does this resonate with anything in your life right now: a new job, new stage, new way of serving God and others?

John 1:35-43; Luke 5:1-11; Matthew 4:18-30; 9:9; Mark 1:16-18

The Call of the Apostles

Words of St. Ignatius

Point One: It seems that St. Peter and St. Andrew were called three times; first, to some knowledge, as is evident from St. John [1:35-42]; second, to follow Christ to some extent, but with an intention to return to the possession of what they had left behind, as St. Luke tells us [5:1-11]; third, to follow Christ our Lord forever [St. Matthew 4:18-30; St. Mark 1:16-18].

Point Two: He called Philip [St. John 1:43], and Matthew, as St. Matthew himself tells us [9:9].

Point Three: He called the other Apostles, although the Gospels do not mention the particular instances.

Three other things too should be considered: first, how they came from a rude and lowly condition of living; second, the dignity to which they were so gently called; and third, the gifts and graces by which they were raised above all the Fathers of the New Testament and the Old.

(Spiritual Exercises, 275)

Commentary

As he simply passes by, Jesus' gentle and humble bearing draws people to him. He is the Lamb of God, and his disciples will become those who "follow the Lamb wherever he goes" (Revelation 14:4). "Where do you live?" is a good question to ask Jesus. Listen to the answer: "Come and see" (John 1:35-39).

Jesus calls his followers in various ways. Sometimes his call comes gradually, as if by stages. There may be an initial preparation time of getting familiar with his gestures, words, and way of life. This builds confidence and an interior sense that it is worth leaving everything for him. Then the moment for a definite decision will arrive, and we may hear something like: Now, leave everything and live for the kingdom.

Sometimes, Jesus' call arises out of an encounter with him. It may happen unexpectedly and casually, in ordinary circumstances, but the "Follow me" is clear (John 1:43). There is no room for beating about the bush.

Sometimes, people find Jesus through a friend's invitation. "Come and you will see," Philip urges Nathanael (John 1:46).

Jesus rejects no one. He does not require that his disciples have a glorious past. Fishermen, tax collectors, zealots, people who are without guile and others who are hard and demanding—all of these become his followers. "God is able from these stones to raise up children to Abraham" (Matthew 3:9). He "chose what is low and despised in the world, even things that are not, to bring to nothing things that are, so that no human being might boast in the presence of God" (1 Corinthians 1:28-29).

Jesus will receive everyone as they are. He will make them his intimate friends by having them live with him, by teaching and correcting them with love. He will give them his power and send them out as the Father sent him. He will give them the vitality and assistance of his Spirit. Jesus will enable his unpromising-looking apostles to become the columns, doors, and foundations of the city of God (Revelation 21:10-14).

For Reflection

How have the Lord's invitations come to you in the past? How is he calling you today? How can you respond?

Leaving all things behind means resisting the urge to come back and look for them once you have given them up. In what areas do you find it most challenging to do this? Is the Lord truly your father and brother—your all, in place of all things?

Luke 7:36-50

The Banquet in the House of Simon the Pharisee

Words of St. Ignatius

Point One: Magdalen enters where Christ our Lord is seated at table in the house of the Pharisee. She was bringing an alabaster jar full of ointment.

Point Two: Staying behind the Lord at his feet, she began to wash them with her tears, and to wipe them with the hair of her head. She kissed his feet, and anointed them with ointment.

Point Three: When the Pharisee accuses Magdalen, Christ speaks in her defense: "Many sins are forgiven her, because she has loved much." And he said to the woman: "Your faith has made you safe; go in peace."

(Spiritual Exercises, 282)

Commentary

Jesus ate with publicans and sinners, but also with people who were well placed and well-to-do, like Simon the Pharisee. Jesus did not attend this banquet to gain social approval (his enemies will accuse him of being a glutton—perhaps for accepting invitations like Simon's), much less to amuse himself. He is interested in the salvation of all and loses no opportunity to heal and save. With Jesus, as with the Father, "there is no partiality" (Ephesians 6:9).

The proud Pharisee relies on his own righteousness. He feels himself indebted to no one. He looks down on sinners and cannot comprehend the forgiveness that Jesus offers.

The repentant woman seems to have abundant economic resources, but she wants to use them to honor Jesus in reparation for her sins. Once oriented toward evil, she now shows herself energetically and affectionately resolved toward the good. Just as she anoints Jesus with costly ointment, she anoints all her actions with a piety that makes them priceless. This woman appears to have come to a profound recognition of her misery. Seeing Jesus' radiant generosity and purity, she has determined to love much and well, in reparation for her sins. She will love Jesus where others pay him no attention and will unite herself with those who follow him to the cross.

The Heart of Jesus praises piety and mercy: the ties of goodness.... "Go in peace."

For Reflection

Consider Jesus, who knows how to reach out to people as different as Simon the Pharisee and the sinful woman. He does not denounce, but tactfully suggests. He brings light lovingly into each heart through his loving questions. What light is Jesus bringing into your heart as you ponder this gospel scene?

When have you received God's forgiveness in an especially powerful way? Did being forgiven motivate and energize you to love Jesus more wholeheartedly?

The woman expressed her repentance with concrete actions. What might you do to express your own sorrow for sin?

Talk over your concerns with the Good Shepherd, and ask him to show you his heart of love.

Matthew 14:22-33; John 6:15-21

Christ on the Waves

Words of St. Ignatius

Point One: While Christ our Lord remained on the mountain, he ordered his disciples to go before him in the little boat. Then he dismissed the multitude and began to pray alone.

Point Two: The little boat was tossed by the waves. Christ came toward it, walking on the waters; and the disciples thought they saw a ghost.

Point Three: Christ said to them, "It is I, do not fear." At his command St. Peter came to him, walking on the water. He doubted, and began to sink. But Christ our Lord saved him, and reprehended him for his little faith. Then he entered into the boat and the wind ceased.

(Spiritual Exercises, 280)

Commentary

Jesus has just multiplied five loaves and two fish into a meal for more than five thousand people. He could have basked in the crowd's praises but resists this temptation to worldly glory and power. He sends his disciples off in the boat and goes *alone* to the mountain to pray.

Who understood what he was doing? Perhaps the disciples felt slighted or perplexed at being dismissed. But Jesus' prayer is no escape. It expresses his firm adherence to the Father's plan for him. The crowd lacks this supernatural vision of life and often has other agendas that Jesus must purify: "Do not labor for the food which perishes, but for the food which endures to eternal life" (John 6:27).

We see the disciples in the boat without Jesus, tossed about by the waves, without the positions they might have hoped for in Jesus' kingdom. But Jesus does not abandon his own forever in their struggle with the waves, and he comes to them over the water. In the darkness of the night, his disciples take him for a ghost. Similarly, our own faith in Jesus must pass through the "dark night" of the senses and powers of the soul (memory, understanding, and will) if it is to be purified.

The Lord's words are effective and bring about what they declare: "Come," says Jesus, and Peter steps out of the boat. But what happens when faith dwindles? Like Peter, we begin to sink! We hear the reproach of Jesus: "You of little faith, why did you doubt?"

Jesus is always faithful. We can count on it. He extends his hand to Peter and invites him to confirm his brothers in their own faith.

The faith, the ship of Peter, Jesus with us—these are the things that last. The waves that toss our little boat will pass. Each storm is a temporary episode. Only God endures and does not change.

For Reflection

As I consider the example of Jesus going off alone to pray, what is God telling me about my own prayer life?

Neither night nor the waves are too much for the Lord to handle. Do I believe this? Does it affect how I approach the dark and stormy periods that come up in my life?

When Jesus asks me "Why do you doubt?" how do I answer?

I join with the apostles in worshiping the Master of wind and sea. "Truly you are the Son of God," and I ask him to calm my troubled waters and to help me receive that peace which the world does not know.

John 11:1-46

The Resurrection of Lazarus

Words of St. Ignatius

Point One: Martha and Mary inform Christ our Lord about the illness of Lazarus. After he heard this news he remained where he was for two days, to make the miracle more evident.

Point Two: Before raising him he asks the two sisters to believe, saying: "I am the resurrection and the life; those who believe in me, even though they die, will live."

Point Three: He raises him, after he has wept and prayed; and the manner in which he raised him was by his command: "Lazarus, come forth."

(Spiritual Exercises, 285)

Commentary

See the disciples and observe their fear at returning to Judea, where Jesus has enemies. Hear their conversation with the Master about the case of Lazarus. How slow they are to grasp the situation! What a contrast with Jesus, who sees the Father's higher purposes and serenely sets out to fulfill them.

A beautiful petition underlies Martha and Mary's message about their brother's death. But why does Jesus delay in responding? Consider the mystery hidden in the test of faith to which he submits his followers. For Jesus, faith is more precious than life. His actions are "so that you may believe," he tells the apostles—and believing, see "the glory of God" (John 11:15,40).

Sense the light, freedom, and security of the heart of Christ. How easily he moves in the midst of the darkness and weakness of the other hearts around him. The presence of death cannot destroy his hope for life.

Pay attention to the firmness and certainty with which Jesus speaks of himself. "I am the resurrection and the life. Those who believe in me, even though they die, will live, and everyone who lives and believes in me will never die" (John 11:25-26). No one in their right mind would make such affirmations seriously. Either Jesus is crazy or he really is the Son of God!

Jesus weeps before the tomb of Lazarus. In his humanity, he is profoundly moved. Stand with Jesus and, with the light of his Spirit, try to explore the reasons for his deep inner distress.

Try to hear and see Jesus as he looks upward and prays aloud: "Father, I thank you for having heard me. I knew that you always hear me, but I have said this for the sake of the crowd standing here, so that they may believe that you sent me" (John 11:41-42).

Reflect on the different reactions of the people after the miracle of Jesus. Reading Jesus' words joins you to this crowd. Are they having the effect Jesus intended?

For Reflection

Consider and reflect on the reactions of all those present at the raising of Lazarus: the disciples, Martha, Mary, the family friends who had come to express their condolences, people hostile to Jesus, Lazarus.

Linger over Martha's statement of faith and make it your own:

"Yes, Lord, I believe that you are the Christ, the Son of God, he who is coming into the world" (John 11:27).

Notice the aspects of this Gospel scene that touch you most intensely. Dwell on them and return to them in order to gain that inner knowledge of Christ which will inspire you to love and follow him more closely.

End with a colloquy.

In Him

Step Three

the fullness of the Paschal mystery

Meditating on Christ's Passion and Death

The paschal mystery reaches its fullness in us only as we die and rise with Christ. The grace we have been asking for—to love and follow Christ more closely—must bring us to identify with him in his suffering and death. Then, incorporated in Christ, we can participate in the glory of his resurrection: " ... provided we suffer with him in order that we may also be glorified with him" (Romans 8:17).

If disordered love is the main obstacle to our discerning how we can best work for the greater service of God, it is our own inner resistance that presents the greatest difficulty in our accomplishing God's will once we discover it. We find this resistance in our sensuality and attachment to comfort, in our drive to set ourselves up well, and in our tendency to compromise with "the world."

But all faithful followers of Christ must choose another course and prepare themselves to face opposition, persecution, mockery, and even hatred. By embracing these and all other forms of suffering entailed in fidelity to the Master, we fulfill the part assigned to us in completing "Christ's afflictions for the sake of his body, that is, the church" (Colossians 1:24). The exercises that follow—contemplations of the Passion and death of our Lord—are directed toward obtaining this fruit.

More deeply than ever before, we will delve into the mystery of Christ the Redeemer, who was sacrificed for our sins so that we might have abundant life. We want to obtain a living realization of this mystery by contemplating it with the help of the Holy Spirit within us. Christ takes our iniquities upon himself and pays the price for our offenses. He makes his offering voluntarily, with full awareness (see Isaiah 53:5-7). Our contemplation means not remaining a spectator but identifying with Christ out of desire to become incorporated in him in the mystery of the Church. We must seek the grace to feel *sorrow with Christ in sorrow; a broken spirit with Christ so broken; tears; and interior suffering because of the great suffering which Christ endured for me* (*Spiritual Exercises*, 203). Here it is not enough to be a sympathetic bystander: We must consider the sufferings of Christ to be our own and accept our share in them.

For Reflection

Jesus immersed himself in the depths of sorrow, humiliation, loneliness, and the most complete spiritual abandonment, and "he learned obedience through what he suffered" (Hebrews 5:8). Seeing what Christ suffered for my sake, I ask myself: *What ought I to do and suffer for him?* (*Spiritual Exercises*, 197).

Meditate on how, in the Passion of Christ, his divinity hides itself—*how he could destroy his enemies but does not so, and how he allows his most holy humanity to suffer so cruelly* (*Spiritual Exercises*, 196). He does so for me.

John 13; Luke 22:14-20; 1 Corinthians 11:23-29

The Last Supper

Words of St. Ignatius

After the usual *preparatory prayer, survey the history* of what you are about to contemplate: *how Christ our Lord sent two disciples from Bethany to Jerusalem to prepare the supper, and later went there himself with his other disciples; and how, after eating the Paschal Lamb and finishing the meal, he washed their feet and gave his Most Holy Body and Precious Blood to his disciples; and further, how he addressed his farewell discourse to them, after Judas had left to sell his Lord.*

Imagine the place: *See in imagination the road from Bethany to Jerusalem, whether it is broad, or narrow, or level, and so on. In similar manner, imagine the room of the supper, whether it is large, or small, or arranged in one way or another.*

Ask for what you desire: *Here it will be to ask for sorrow, regret, and confusion, because the Lord is going to his Passion for my sins.*

Reflect on the Last Supper, as St. Ignatius suggests in the six "points" for this exercise:

Point One: to see the persons at the supper; and then, by reflecting on myself, to endeavor to draw some profit from them.

Point Two: to listen to what they are saying, and similarly to draw profit from that.

Point Three: to see what they are doing, and to draw profit from it.

Point Four: Consider what Christ our Lord suffers in his human nature, or desires to suffer.... Then one should begin here with much effort to bring oneself to grief, sorrow, and tears, and in this same manner to work through the points which follow.

Point Five: Consider how his divinity hides itself; that is, how he could destroy his enemies but does not, and how he allows his most holy humanity to suffer so cruelly.

Point Six: Consider how he suffers all this for my sins, and so on; and also ask: What ought I do and suffer for him?

Finish with a colloquy to Christ our Lord, and at its end recite an Our Father.

(Spiritual Exercises, 190-198)

For Reflection

Before you begin this exercise, be sure to read the accounts of the Last Supper in John 13, Luke 22:14-20, and 1 Corinthians 13:23-29. What particular insight does each passage contribute to your understanding of the scene?

Commentary

This mystery of Jesus at the Last Supper, where he washes his disciples' feet and institutes the Eucharist, is especially rich and lends itself to many varied emphases. In the *Spiritual Exercises*, the scene has particular significance as a prelude to Christ's suffering and death. St. Ignatius invites us to see the gestures and words of Jesus during the supper as marked by the Passion that is already reverberating in our Savior's heart, and he directs us to ask for *sorrow, regret, and confusion, because the Lord is going to his Passion for my sins* (*Spiritual Exercises*, 193).

The account of the Last Supper in John 13 helps guide the contemplation from this perspective. Even in its first verses, the sin of betrayal that is about to trigger the Passion hangs over the scene like an immense weight (John 13:2-3). Christ's heaviness of heart is evident in his words and is revealed unexpectedly from the conversation. The sin of Judas is described as a stain (13:11), trampling Jesus underfoot (13:18), a betrayal (13:1,18,21,); it is Satan's entrance into the sinner, a sinking into the shadows of night (13:27,30). But throughout all this, the paschal consciousness of Jesus shines out before our eyes. He knows that the hour of his passing from the world to the Father has arrived, that he came from the Father and is now returning to him (13:1,3), that he is establishing a kingdom where we will have a place with him (13:8,19,32,33,36).

Observe the final manifestations of the love of Jesus. See how he humbles himself at the feet of each disciple—even the traitor—in a supreme gesture of self-offering for their redemption. "I have given you an example, that you should do as I have done to you. . . . If you know these things, blessed are you if you do them" ((John 13:15,17). How eloquently Christ's example reinforces his recommendations of mutual humility and loving service! "Now is the Son of man glorified, and in him God is glorified" (13:31).

Let us try to resonate with the beating of Christ's heart in his living sacrifice: "This is the new covenant in my blood" (Luke 22:20). How eagerly he has awaited this moment for celebrating the Passover with his disciples (22:15)! Jesus is now the true Lamb who takes away the sin of the world. The image gives way to the reality it signifies. The Old Covenant gives way to the new: "Sacrifices and offerings you have not desired, but a body you have prepared for me . . . See, God, I have come to do your will" (Hebrews 10:5-7).

Linger over the account of this first Eucharist in 1 Corinthians 11:23-29. Here, Christ instituted the priesthood, with all its consequences. He willed to place himself in so many hands—even hands recently stained by sin—and to make himself vulnerable to human beings prone to caprice, irreverence, and sacrilege. But none of this could deter his loving desire to make himself food for his creatures. Now this incomprehensible love of Jesus reaches out to enkindle our own.

For Reflection

What aspects of Jesus' words and actions at the Last Supper do I find most moving? Why?

What have I learned during this exercise that can help me to grow in appreciating the Eucharist and approaching it more reverently? How can I implement this in my life?

How have these mysteries awakened in me the desire to participate in the Passion to which the Lord is going in order to redeem me from my sins?

Luke 22:39-47; Matthew 26:30-46; Mark 14:26-42

The Agony in the Garden

Words of St. Ignatius

After the usual *preparatory prayer*, I will think about *how Christ our Lord descended with his eleven disciples from Mt. Sion, where the supper had been eaten, into the Valley of Jehoshaphat. He left eight of them in one part of the valley and three in an area of the garden. He began to pray, and his sweat became like drops of blood. After he had prayed three times to his Father and awakened his disciples, his enemies fell back at his words. Then Judas gave him the kiss of peace and St. Peter cut off the ear of Malchus, but Christ put it back in place. He was arrested as a malefactor, and his captors led him down the valley and up its other side to the house of Annas.*

I will imagine the place—here, *the road from Mt. Zion down into the Valley of Jehoshaphat, and the Garden, whether it is small or large, whether of one appearance or another.*

I will *ask for what I desire. Here it is what is proper for the Passion: sorrow with Christ in sorrow; a broken spirit with Christ so broken; tears; and interior suffering because of the great suffering which Christ endured for me....*

Point One: Our Lord, after finishing the supper and singing a hymn, went to Mount Olivet with his disciples, who were full of fear. He left eight of them in Gethsemane, and said, "Sit here while I go over there and pray."

Point Two: Accompanied by St. Peter, St. James, and St. John, he prayed three times to the Lord, saying, "My Father, if it is possible, let this cup pass from me; yet, not as I will, but as you will." And being in agony, he prayed the longer.

Point Three: He came to a fear so great that he said, "My soul is sorrowful even unto death," and he sweated blood so copiously that St. Luke says, "His sweat became like drops of blood falling on the ground." This supposes that his clothes were already full of blood.

(Spiritual Exercises, 201-203,290)

Commentary

"And when they had sung a hymn, they went out . . ." (Matthew 26:30). Not a single prescription of the Law is left unfulfilled by Jesus, even in these circumstances. The hymns he sang with his disciples were Psalms 113–118, which closed the celebration of the Passover meal: "I do as the Father has commanded me, so that the world may know that I love the Father. Rise, let us go hence" (John 14:31).

In your contemplation, accompany the group of disciples as they go down with the Master to the Kidron stream. Listen as Peter protests, "Even if I must die with you . . ." (Matthew 26:35), entering into his sentiments and trying to fathom those in the heart of Christ. Feel the waves of trepidation that expand among the disciples, who are moved to sadness as the tone of events and the Master's words become ever more somber: "You will all fall away because of me this night" (26:31).

Watch and pray. Stay here and watch: "Pray that you may not enter into temptation" (Luke 22:40). It is good to stand very close to Jesus—inside his heart, if possible—as you contemplate his agony. The hour has come to identify yourself with his sacrifice. "He began to be sorrowful and troubled" (Matthew 26:37). Christ allows immense waves of sadness to penetrate his inner self—caused by the hardening of his enemies' hearts, the murder which they are about to commit, the betrayal of Judas, the denial of Peter, abandonment by all. He sees ahead to the many people who will ignore his suffering and death, coldly neglecting and denying him and dying unrepentant and condemned.

Jesus "began to be greatly distressed . . ." (Mark 14:33)—to feel confusion, weakness, interior collapse. The Passion hovers over him like an immense phantom: "Many bulls encompass me . . . they open wide their mouths at me, like a ravening and roaring lion. . . . Yea, dogs are round about me: a company of evildoers encircles me: they have pierced my hands and feet—I can count all my bones" (Psalm 22:12-13,16-17). Even though Jesus has not yet physically experienced all this, his imagination makes all his sufferings present.

". . . and troubled" (Mark 14:33)—that is, drained of vigor and attacked by nausea, discouragement, revulsion. Jesus feels an interior disintegration so intense that it brings him to fall face down, limp, sweating blood. "My heart is like wax, it is melted within my breast; my strength is dried up like a potsherd, and my tongue cleaves to my jaws; you lay me in the dust of death" (Psalm 22:14-15). Who would dare to reprove him by saying that a man must face sorrow and death courageously? "But I am a worm, and no man; scorned by men, and despised by the people" (22:6). Jesus has become the living representation of the sin of the world before the divine justice.

Jesus insisted again and again in his prayer: "Not what I want but what you want, Father; not my will but yours be done." At the height of his desolation he prolonged his prayer: one hour, two, three. Meanwhile the disciples were dozing, overcome by sleep.

The fruit of the prayer of Jesus was not consolation, but strength. Serenely and firmly, with decisive love, he put himself into the hands of his enemies so that the sacrifice desired by the Father might be fulfilled in him. He accepted the cup of suffering, making it the cup of our salvation.

For Reflection

Do I struggle to avoid every suffering? How often do I refuse to endure even small inconveniences or hurts for the sake of Jesus? What must I do to open myself to that love of Christ which will enable me to endure trials patiently for the greater glory of God and the good of my neighbor?

Where in my life is it hardest for me to say, "Not what I want, Father. Not my will but yours be done"?

Matthew 26:47-68; Luke 22:47-65; Mark 14:42-72; John 18:1-27

Jesus Is Arrested and Condemned

Words of St. Ignatius

Our Lord allowed himself to be kissed by Judas, and to be arrested as a thief by the crowd, to whom he said, "You have come out as against a robber with swords and clubs to seize me. Day after day I was teaching in the temple, and you did not arrest me." And when he asked, "Whom are you seeking?" his enemies fell to the ground.

St. Peter wounded a servant of the high priest; and the meek Lord said to him, "Put your sword back into its sheath." Then he healed the servant's wound.

Abandoned by his disciples, he is dragged before Annas, where St. Peter, who had followed him from afar, denied him once, and a blow was given to Christ by a servant who said to him, "Is this the way you answer the high priest?"

They take him bound from the house of Annas to that of Caiaphas, where St. Peter denied him twice. When our Lord looked at him, he went out and wept bitterly.

Jesus remained bound all that night.

Besides this, those who held him prisoner mocked him, struck him, blindfolded him, slapped him, and asked him: "Prophesy for us: Who it is that struck you?" They also uttered similar blasphemies against him.

(Spiritual Exercises, 291-292)

Commentary

"Would you betray the Son of Man with a kiss?" (Luke 22:48). Imagine Jesus' look as he puts this question to Judas.

"I am he" (John 18:5). Jesus offers himself for his friends and even for his enemies. He does this willingly and wholeheartedly, knowing it will cost him his life, and not like someone who hopes to escape.

- Accompany Jesus dragged about as an evildoer. Observe how he is abandoned by his disciples. Ponder the injustice and uncontrolled violence directed against him: slaps, blows, public humiliation before some of the very people who had acclaimed him with hosannas as the one sent in the name of the Lord. Unite yourself with Jesus' attitude of perfect offering.

- "If I have spoken rightly, why do you strike me?" (John 18:23). Explore the meaning of salvation in this question, so full of pity and love. Jesus desires to save even his enemies. Even in this abusive situation, Jesus does not accuse. With sober serenity and self-control, he offers a question that invites the sinner to recognize his error and take the opportunity to repent. Notice Jesus' silences as well as his responses; he uses each not to defend himself, but to reach out to those who have wronged him.

- Accompany Jesus bound all the night. Those who held him prisoner mocked him: "Prophesy for us: who is it that struck you?" (Matthew 26:68).

For Reflection

- "Would you betray me with a kiss?. . . I am he. . . Why do you strike me?. . ."

The Passion accounts are rich in thought-provoking statements. Choose one to mull over in Jesus' presence, and jot down some of your thoughts about it. Give freedom to your feelings to participate in the sufferings and humiliations of Christ.

Consider the enormity of this event: God is condemned by his creatures, who resent his interfering with their plans. Thank Jesus for his valiant and decisive confession before Caiaphas (Matthew 26:63-64).

Matthew 27:1-26; Luke 23:1-12; Mark 15:1-15

Jesus Is Sentenced to Death

Words of St. Ignatius

The whole multitude of the Jews bring Christ to Pilate, and before him they accuse him, saying: "We have found this man misleading our people. He forbids payment of taxes to Caesar."

Pilate, after having examined him again and again, says, "I find no guilt in him."

Barabbas the robber was preferred before him. "They cried: 'Not this man, but Barabbas.'"

Pilate sent Jesus the Galilean to Herod, the tetrarch of Galilee.

Through curiosity Herod questioned him at length, but he gave no answer, even though the scribes and priests unceasingly accused him.

(Spiritual Exercises, 293-294)

Commentary

Thanks to the cowardice of Pilate and Herod, who shirk their responsibilities, Jesus becomes a pawn in the political game. What a contrast there is between these spiritually blind and frivolous rulers and the calm, self-possessed King of kings!

Notice that Jesus says not a word to Herod. Herod mocks and shows contempt for the one who is a living reproach to him by his silence and modesty.

Note Pilate's behavior as well. He declares Jesus innocent up to six times but confirms his condemnation nonetheless. What impressive inconsistency this coward shows! "I did not find this man guilty of any of your charges against him," Pilate says. But he adds, "I will therefore chastise him and release him" (Luke 23:14,16; also 22). Under pressure, he caves in.

The crowd demands the release of the criminal Barabbas. How can they put Jesus on the same level as Barabbas! But what about me? What have I put up as a rival to Jesus? Friends, position, reputation, social pressure, work, agendas of one kind or another?

For Reflection

With the Spirit's help, try to put yourself in the place of Pilate, of Herod, and of the crowd. Have you ever acted out of the motives that led them to do what they did?

Seek to enter into the Heart of Jesus at the moment he receives the sentence. It is *my* shame, *my* suffering—but Jesus accepts without resentment. Wholeheartedly, he submits to the Father's will with a burning desire to complete his mission and reveal his love. And all that for me.

Mark 15:15-20

Jesus Is Scourged and Crowned with Thorns

Words of St. Ignatius

Meanwhile: *Pilate took Jesus, and scourged him. Then the soldiers wove a crown out of thorns, and placed it on his head, and they clothed him in a purple cloak; and they came before him and said, "Hail, king of the Jews!" And they struck him repeatedly.*

(Spiritual Exercises, 295)

Commentary

I will make myself present to hear the ferocious blows falling upon the holy body of Jesus and to see and feel how his skin turns color, opens up, and bleeds profusely. Behind each blow, I will discover the spirit of oblation and offering of Jesus. He accepted all this for me, so that I might be pure, holy, and immaculate in his presence and live with him forever. What can I offer Jesus in return?

Let us be "always carrying in the body the death of Jesus, so that the life of Jesus may also be manifested in our bodies" (2 Corinthians 4:10). See Jesus lying exhausted in a pool of blood, and there, next to his fallen body, offer him your plan of personal reform. What do you think is his response?

Jesus the King is mocked—given a reed for a scepter, a scarlet cloak, a bundle of thorns for a crown. Delivered over to the vilest sentiments of the human heart, he triumphs over human pride.

When I look at you, Jesus, how can I not feel ashamed to clothe myself in finery? When I see the crown of thorns pressing down on your temples, I search my heart to discover what desires for earthly triumph and importance I still cherish in my inner self. What fear of ridicule prevents me from giving you my all?

The soldiers knelt down in jeering homage to you, my Lord. When I see their mocking genuflections, it awakens my desire to make reparation to you. Teach me to come before you in spirit and truth, with a deep sense of adoration and reverence.

For Reflection

Christ's Passion continues. It must be completed in his body, in the life of the Church, in all of us. Invite the Holy Spirit to help you explore this great mystery and its meaning for your life.

What should I do and suffer for Christ?

John 19:13-37

They Led Him Away to Crucify Him

Words of St. Ignatius

Pilate, seated like a judge, handed Jesus over to be crucified, after the Jews had denied him as their king: "We have no king but Caesar."

He carried the cross on his shoulders, and as he could not carry it, Simon of Cyrene was compelled to carry it behind Jesus.

They crucified him in the middle between two thieves, and placed this title above him: "Jesus of Nazareth, King of the Jews."

He spoke seven words on the cross; he prayed for those who were crucifying him; he forgave the thief; he commended St. John to his mother and his mother to St. John; he said with a loud voice, "I thirst," and they gave him gall and vinegar, he said that he was forsaken; he said, "It is finished"; he said, "Father, into your hands I commend my spirit."

The sun was darkened, the rocks were split, the tombs were opened, the veil of the temple was torn in two from top to bottom.

They blaspheme him, saying, "You who would destroy the temple of God, come down from the cross." His garments were divided. His side was pierced by the lance, and water and blood flowed out.

(Spiritual Exercises, 296-97)

Commentary

"So that the world may know that I love the Father" (John 14:31), Jesus embraced the wood of the cross. By one tree, death came to us; by another will come life.

Simon was compelled to carry the cross with Jesus. What an unexpected blessing! St. Bernard of Clairvaux said that "the beginner in the fear of God carries the cross with patience; one who has advanced in hope carries it with pleasure; but he who has a consummate love, embraces it passionately" (*Sermon on St. Andrew*, 5). Have I learned something in this school of the wisdom of the cross? Do I confuse the way that leads to God with the way of earthly success, or can I see it as the way that leads to the apparent ruin of Calvary?

Jesus appreciates the compassion of the women who weep over him but points out the true cause for tears: "Weep for yourselves and for your children. . . . For if they do this when the wood is green, what will happen when it is dry?" (Luke 23:28,31). It is sin that must be wept over.

At the end, Jesus is lifted up on the cross, which becomes the ladder between heaven and earth. Jesus reigns. Immediately he offers words of pardon for those who have crucified him. He admits a repentant criminal into his kingdom: "Today you will be with me in Paradise" (Luke 23:43). Through it all, Jesus hears the rising tone of taunts: "He saved others; he cannot save himself. . . . Let him come down now from the cross, and we will believe in him" ((Matthew 27:42). They wound him in his deepest sentiments: "He trusts in God; let God deliver him now, if he loves him; for he said, 'I am the son of God'" (27:43).

Hear Jesus' words of pardon and surrender. He gives us everything he has—even his blessed mother. "Behold, your mother!" (John 19:27).

"I thirst," Jesus says so that the Scriptures might be fulfilled (John 19:28). And he is given vinegar to drink. Participate in Jesus' supreme humiliation: He is the object of ridicule—cruelly taunted by the crowd and the authorities as the soldiers cast lots over his clothes. People gloat over him as someone defeated and squashed underfoot. All of this Jesus undergoes with complete personal abandonment.

No one could ever comprehend the mystery of what Jesus suffered in that last instant of earthly life. In the end, he feels abandoned even by his Father: "My God, my God, why have you forsaken me?" (Matthew 27:46). This is the deepest mystery of his Passion. Perhaps the only way to get some slight insight into it is through the experience of someone who has passed through deep trials of purification in the area of their faith. Probably there is no more agonizing suffering in human earthly existence, nothing which so shakes a person down to the very foundations.

Having accomplished everything, Jesus abandons himself totally into the hands of the Father. "And he bowed his head and gave up his spirit" (John 19:30). In a certain sense, the cross signifies a break with what the world considers reasonable. It invites us to ascend to a level beyond what seems possible for human feet to reach. Human prudence—not wanting to risk any goods

at hand for an uncertain future—finds it absurd.
And yet, the cross attracts. "And I, when I am lifted up from the earth, will draw all men to myself" (John 12:32). Consider, in an attitude of adoration, how the depths of humiliation and the beginnings of exaltation coincide: nature weeps, the veil of the temple is rent, the tombs open up, the centurion praises God, the multitudes beat their breasts (Luke 23:44-48).

The cross unites heaven and earth. With open arms, it blesses and teaches the road to victory. The cross demonstrates to us how far our sin has gone and how far the love of God has stretched.

For Reflection

Choose one of the following Scripture passages. With desire to assimilate the wisdom of the cross into your ordinary life, let the Scripture guide you into a prayer of praise, adoration, repentance, and thanksgiving:

Christ "emptied himself, taking the form of a servant, being born in the likeness of men. And being found in human form he humbled himself and became obedient unto death, even death on a cross. Therefore God has highly exalted him and bestowed on him the name which is above every name, that at the name of Jesus every knee should bow, in heaven and on earth and under the earth, and every tongue confess that Jesus Christ is Lord, to the glory of God the Father" (Philippians 2:7-11).

"For if while we were enemies we were reconciled to God by the death of his Son, much more, now that we are reconciled, shall we be saved by his life" (Romans 5:10).

The next two exercises explore aspects of the Passion, taken as a whole. Their purpose is to help you enter into Christ's suffering so that you can appreciate it more deeply and respond to it with greater generosity.

As part of your contemplation of these mysteries, it would be good to read and quietly reflect on one of the four gospel accounts of the Passion. Meditate on the Passion as a whole, and accompany Our Lady in her sorrows and in her solitude.

Christ's Sufferings and Humiliations

Commentary

This meditation summarizes the physical pains, interior sufferings, and humiliations that Jesus experienced in his Passion. With this evidence of his love impressed on my soul, what can deter me in my desire to respond with love in return?

Physical pains: emotional exhaustion, distress, fatigue, prostration, sweating of blood; slaps and blows, lack of sleep through the night, hunger, thirst, scourging, loss of blood, open wounds, falls under the weight of the cross, physical collapse; the nails, tension on nerves and tendons, suffocation, oppression. . . .

Interior sufferings: foreknowledge of what was about to take place, anxiety, sorrow, terror, fear, annihilation, the abandonment and incomprehension of others, betrayal by intimate friends; the eternal loss of those who set themselves obstinately against God, the blasphemies of his enemies; the oppression of being circled around by unbridled evil, treacherous plots, hypocrisies, the power of darkness; the scattering of his flock, the sorrow of his mother, the final sense of abandonment by his Father. . . .

Humiliations of many kinds and degrees: weakness, exhaustion, being submerged and brought down to the ground in the most abject prostration, as a worm and not a man; being undone, made the living representation of human sin, seemingly rejected by his Father. . . .

Disrespectful and abusive treatment as a criminal, a prisoner—dragged and shoved about, the object of blows, slaps, spitting, and taunts from the people, soldiers, executioners and authorities; rejection in favor of a cruel thief and criminal; charged with being a rioter and deceiver of the multitudes, and, most painful of all, condemned for blaspheming. . . .

The total rejection of his claim to be the Messiah, the dispersion of his followers, the fickleness of the people who turn their backs on him after acclaiming him only days before; the seemingly complete failure of his work and appearance of utter defeat before the whole world; the victorious fury of his raging enemies; his lonely death, with no one to defend him....

For Reflection

To what extent do I try to hide from the cross of Christ? Am I deceiving myself about this? Perhaps there is a particular suffering that I don't want to call a cross and try to escape from. Perhaps I feel bitter even thinking about it.

Lord, help me to open my eyes once and for all. Help me to discover in my most difficult situations the blessing of the cross with its abundance of graces. Lord, make me willing to suffer everything for love of you.

The Passion in the Senses of Christ

Commentary

Consider the suffering Jesus experienced:

Through his eyes: heaviness, sleepiness, tears; the unfolding sight of a degrading, cruel, and humiliating spectacle full of dark plots, spiritual blindness, cowardice, instigations, shadows, darkness. . . .

Through his ears: shouting, cries of anger, incoherent words, false accusations, blasphemies, inciting whispers, absurd conclusions, mockeries, sardonic remarks. . . .
Through his sense of smell: the odor of filth, dampness, stale air, and sweat; of base and lurid vice, of corrupt minds and hearts full of treason and malice. . . .

Through his sense of taste: the bitterness of abandonment and betrayal, acrid tears mixed with saliva and blood, hunger, terrible thirst caused by the great loss of blood, the choking sensation from swallowed dust and dirt. . . .

Through his sense of touch: the racing pulse and pressure, the tension of muscles and nerves, severe fatigue and weariness, the pain of blows, bruises, wounds, a throbbing in the temples, the final collapse—respiratory failure and final suffocation. . . .

Jesus endured all this and more with the greatest patience and compassion. His understanding eyes swept the crowd with a merciful gaze that elicited Peter's repentance, looked generously upon John, and united him intimately as son with his sorrowful mother. Jesus raised those eyes in ardent petition to the Father, asking pardon for his assassins. He looked ahead to far horizons, offering hope and encouragement to those who weep for him.

Humble, in control of himself, and majestically silent when need be, Jesus also offered measured words that could penetrate hearts and pour out salvation even when he was on the cross. Now too, Jesus has ears that are attentive to even the slightest hint of a sincere question, the slightest opening to conversion. He knows how to forget what he has heard, how to rise above offenses to resonate with the petition of the repentant sinner.

Jesus "gave himself up for us, a fragrant offering and sacrifice to God" (Ephesians 5:2). With absolute abandon, he gave himself over into the arms of the Father. He drew all things to himself in the kiss of justice and peace.

For Reflection

This meditation aims to help transform the senses by uniting them to those of Christ in his Passion. As with the preceding contemplations of these sorrowful mysteries, make your prayer of petition be for sorrow with Christ in sorrow and for brokenness with Christ broken.

"And no one will take your joy from you." (John 16:22)

Meditating on Christ's Passion and death required us to confront our inner resistance to suffering. Contemplating the risen Christ also presents a difficulty. Only with great effort can our human nature rise above disordered self-love and escape to identify with another in his victory. But while it is important to have suffered with Christ in his Passion, it is also important, if perhaps more difficult, to feel as our own the joy and happiness of Christ raised from the dead. In the contemplations that follow, therefore, we are going to ask for *the grace to be glad and to rejoice intensely because of the great glory and joy of Christ our Lord*, now risen and triumphant (*Spiritual Exercises*, 221).

Alluding to both the challenge and the rightness of rejoicing, St. Augustine wrote: "Before Easter, we celebrate what we are also experiencing. After Easter, on the other hand, what we are celebrating, which we express with signs, we do not yet possess. That is why in the former time we exercise ourselves in fasting and in prayer; while now, we leave behind the fasting, and dedicate ourselves to praise" ("Expositions on the Psalms," 148,1).

Our contemplations of the Passion put us in contact with the hard realities entailed in following Christ. Contemplating the resurrection aims to make us conscious that in our sufferings, we have the comforting presence of the glorified Christ, who brings joy, grace, and the hope of the eternal life already begun in us. While his presence is often not something we perceive or see as enjoyable in ourselves, it is a real and authentic gift that the Lord offers. Every day, he invites us to enter more deeply into the joy of knowing that he is with us.

Practical Helps

In the exercises that follow, use the same procedure as in previous contemplations (see pages 83 and 91). Additionally, St. Ignatius advises, keep these goals in mind:

- Consider how the divinity of Christ, which seemed to hide itself in the Passion, now makes its presence marvelously known in the mysteries of the risen Christ (*Spiritual Exercises*, 223);
- Recognize Christ's role as consoler in these mysteries. He reaches out *the way friends console one another* (*Spiritual Exercises*, 224).

St. Ignatius also offers very concrete recommendations about the physical environment for meditating on the resurrection. Take advantage of good weather, have your prayer room brightly lit, pursue thoughts of joy, and reduce penances. All of this, he says, can help you better rejoice in the Lord.

Of course, Ignatius is not encouraging the superficial, raucous partying that often passes for joy in this world. He wishes to help us seek something deeper, more transcendent and uplifting: participation in the joy of the risen Christ, which comes as a precious gift from above, from the Father of lights, from whom comes "every perfect gift" (James 1:17).

1 Corinthians 15:42-58; 1 Peter 1:3-9

The Resurrection of Christ and His Appearance to Our Lady

Part of this contemplation involves a scene that the gospels do not mention: Christ's post-resurrection appearance to his mother. *Although this is not stated in Scripture*, says St. Ignatius, *still it is considered as understood by the statement that he appeared to many others* (see Acts 13:31; 1 Corinthians 15:6). Such a scene only make sense, Ignatius implies: *For Scripture supposes that we have understanding, as it is written: "Are even you without understanding?"* (Matthew 15:16) (*Spiritual Exercises*, 299).

Words of St. Ignatius

After the *preparatory prayer*, consider the *history*, or overview, of this mystery. *Here it is how, after Christ died on the cross, his body remained separated from his soul but always united with his divinity. His blessed soul, also united with his divinity, descended to hell. Then releasing the souls of the just from there, returning to the sepulcher, and rising again, he appeared in body and soul to his Blessed Mother.*

The place: *See the arrangement of the holy sepulcher; also, the place or house where Our Lady was, including its various parts, such as a room, an oratory, and the like.*

The petition: *It is to ask for what I desire. Here it will be to ask for the grace to be glad and to rejoice intensely because of the great glory and joy of Christ our Lord.*

Points for meditation: As in the exercise on the Last Supper, St. Ignatius says to imaginatively see the persons involved in each scene of meeting with the risen Christ, to listen to what they are saying, and to observe what they are doing—*and then, by reflecting on myself, to draw some profit from them* (*Spiritual Exercises*, 194).

Two additional points: *Consider how the divinity, which seemed hidden during the Passion, now appears and manifests itself so miraculously in this holy Resurrection, through its true and most holy effects. Consider the office of consoler which Christ our Lord carries out, and compare it with the way friends console one another.*

Finish with a colloquy, according to the subject matter, and recite the Our Father.

(Spiritual Exercises, 218-225)

For Reflection

Today is a good time to reflect again on the preparatory prayer and to pray it with special intensity and a yearning for perfect love: *That all my intentions, actions, and operations may be ordered purely to the service and praise of the Divine Majesty* (*Spiritual Exercises*, 46).

Ask the Holy Spirit to show you what you can to do to make your whole life an expression of this prayer.

Commentary

In this contemplation, we visualize three scenes:

The soul of Christ greeting the souls of those who died in the hope of the Redeemer.
A very ancient homily pictures Jesus exhorting Adam: "Awake, you who sleep; I did not create you that you would remain detained in hell. Get up from among the dead, for I am life . . . For you I, your God, made myself your child . . . for you I was crucified" (*Patres Graeci*, t 43,

462 ss). Supported by the article of our faith, "he descended into hell," we also may contemplate in some manner how Christ made himself present to the souls of the just. Observe how, in an instant, all the expectations of so many centuries were fulfilled. Imagine Abraham, who was filled with joy to see the day of the Lord (see John 8:56). Here are Isaac, Moses, the repentant sinner David, and all the prophets who had announced the Messiah's coming. Here are St. Joseph and John the Baptist, Joachim, Anna, Simeon, who contemplated Jesus as the light in his arms. . . .

Jesus frees the just forever from their captivity. The seed that fell into the earth has borne its fruit (John 12:24)! Hear the resounding thanksgiving of this throng, as they adore the price of their salvation! Together with them, reverently kiss the blessed wounds of Christ. "Worthy is the Lamb who was slain, to receive power and wealth and wisdom and might and honor and glory and blessing!" (Revelation 5:12).

The sepulcher containing the body of Our Lord. The moment has arrived. The body which had been placed hurriedly in the tomb—so deformed by wounds, bruises, and blood as to be almost unrecognizable—is suddenly invaded by the triumphant soul of Christ. Gloriously transformed, it overflows with splendor and celestial power. Christ is risen! He has passed into eternity. He retains his real body, but now it is penetrated with spiritual qualities. Freed from the limits of space and time, he can now make himself present wherever and whenever he likes. Distances, walls, and locked doors no longer present the slightest obstacle. "What is sown is perishable, what is raised is imperishable. . . . It is sown a physical body, it is raised a spiritual body" (1 Corinthians 15:42,44).

"The last enemy to be destroyed is death"—but now death has been "swallowed up" in the victory of Christ (1 Corinthians 15:26,55)! Death no longer has dominion over him, or over us either, if we believe in Christ. In the resurrection, human nature has been given new life. This is the day that the Lord has made! This is the joy no one can take from us! For all who unite themselves to Christ in their earthly life, the powers of hell are overthrown forever!

The quiet room in which Our Lady is praying. Church Fathers like St. Ambrose and George of Nicomedia—along with others, including John Paul II—have thought that Our Lady was the first to see the resurrection, since she had also been the first to believe in it. Contemplate this meeting of the Son with his mother. Make yourself present in Our Lady's room, without disturbing her in her prayer.

Scripture portrays Our Lady as a meditating soul. What is she going over in her mind in her solitude, as the risen Jesus draws near to console her and bring her joy? Is she perhaps pondering the terrible scenes of Calvary, the crushed and lifeless figure of her divine Son? Even in her deep grief, Mary has maintained her serene faith in the resurrection of her Son. As the third day draws near, we can imagine her speaking words from the Song of Songs: "Awake, O north wind, and come, O south wind! Blow upon my garden, let its fragrance be wafted abroad. Let my beloved come to his garden, and eat its choicest fruits . . ." (Song 4:16). And we hear Jesus' voice in the reply of the Beloved: "I come to my garden . . . I gather my myrrh with my spice, I eat my honeycomb with my honey. . . . Eat, O friends, and drink: drink deeply" (Song of Songs 5:1).

Ask the Holy Spirit to expand your capacity to feel intimately the immense joy of that meeting. Here is Jesus raised from the dead and glorious before the most pure eyes of his mother. She herself is the most precious fruit of his redemption, and he sees her in all the truth of her sublime interior beauty. Son of God and son of Mary, Jesus alone is capable of appreciating it fully, with the Father and the Spirit.

Rejoice with Jesus, and rejoice with Mary as she contemplates her divine Son present in the splendor of his triumph. This is the Lord of heaven and earth—more resplendent than the sun, radiating forth his sanctifying power. St. Peter forgot himself in an ecstasy of happiness at Mount Tabor, which was only an anticipation of Christ's glorification. What, then, will it be like to see Christ in the fullness of his glorified being?

For Reflection

"When the cares of my heart are many, your consolations cheer my soul" (Psalm 94:19). Consolation, according to St. Ignatius, is *every increase in hope, faith, and charity* (*Spiritual Exercises*, 316). Which "consolations" have you found in this exercise that you want to remember to cheer your soul when the going gets hard or dull?

Luke 24:13-35

The Appearance to the Disciples on the Road to Emmaus

Words of St. Ignatius

Meditate on this encounter with the risen Lord using the following points:

Point One: He appears to the disciples, who were going to Emmaus, and were conversing about Christ.

Point Two: He upbraids them, showing from the Scriptures that Christ had to die and to rise again: "Oh, how foolish you are and slow of heart to believe all the things which the prophets have spoken. Was it not necessary that Christ should suffer these things and thus enter into his glory?"

Point Three: At their urging he remained there and was with them until he gave them Communion and then disappeared. They returned and told the disciples how they had recognized him in the Communion.

(Spiritual Exercises, 303)

Commentary

"Delight your soul and comfort your heart, and remove sorrow far from you, for sorrow has destroyed many, and there is no profit in it" (Sirach 30:23). Watch the disciples walking along sadly. They want to forget everything—to put their troubles behind them and return home to manage their own affairs and to rest. And what about us? How much we, too, suffer from not understanding the cross!

Listen to what the two disciples have been saying about Christ. The dying embers of love are not entirely extinguished. Observe the familiarity with which Christ enters into the conversation, as a good friend would. He speaks and also lets the others speak. He lets them pour out what is on their minds, listening attentively but knowing what to say to bring them around.

Jesus expresses surprise that the two disciples are "slow of heart to believe all that the prophets have spoken!" (Luke 24:25). Why have they not searched the Scriptures? "They bear witness to me," Jesus had once explained (John 5:39). With the light of his Spirit, Jesus is the key to the Scriptures.

The disciples' hearts are burning, though they do not notice right away that the flame has been relit. They are won over by Jesus' friendly and open way with them. "Stay with us" they plead (Luke 24:29). Seeing that they appreciate his presence, he does.

And they recognize him in the breaking of the bread (Luke 24:31). Do the gestures of Jesus which we have contemplated make him familiar to us? They should.

See how the disciples' enthusiasm returns. This is a deep joy based on faith and hope reborn. It flourishes anew with power and vigor under the action of Christ the Lord, the one who triumphs over sin and death and every power of darkness.

Christ's presence brings peace and with it, mutual love and reconciliation. Immediately, the disciples return to the community in Jerusalem to share their joy and their witness.

Jesus does not abandon us: "I will be with you always, to the close of the age" (Matthew 28:20).

For Reflection

Remember the words of Holy Scripture that especially speak to you about friendship with Christ. Use them as part of your personal prayer for a closer walk with the risen Lord.

After Jesus had left them, the disciples said to each other, "Did not our hearts burn within us while he talked to us on the road, while he opened to us the scriptures?" (Luke 24:32). Have you ever sensed Christ with you? What could you do to become more sensitive to his presence? What could you do to discover Christ in the Scriptures?

The resurrection is news too good to keep to ourselves. Take some time to think about how you might encourage other people toward their own personal encounter with the risen Lord.

John 21:1-24

The Appearance at the Lake

Words of St. Ignatius

Point One: Jesus appears to seven of his disciples who were fishing, after they had caught nothing during the whole night. They cast forth the net at his bidding, and "were unable to pull it in because of the number of the fish."

Point Two: Through this miracle St. John recognized him and said to St. Peter, "It is the Lord." Thereupon St. Peter jumped into the sea and came to Christ.

Point Three: He gave them part of a roasted fish and a honeycomb to eat. He asked St. Peter three times about his love for him, and then he entrusted his sheep to him: "Feed my sheep."

(Spiritual Exercises, 306)

Commentary

"I am going fishing," Simon Peter announces, and the other disciples immediately fall in with his plans: "We will go with you" (John 21:3). The mood now is different than before: It is one of peace and harmony. How easily unity builds, when each person embraces the proposals of others with humility.

The disciples go fishing with Peter. It is arduous labor, and throughout that weary night, they catch no fish. Jesus is watching over them, but they are not aware of it. When morning comes, he calls to them from the shore. Jesus is always with the disciples, as he promised (Matthew 28:20), though at times it seems to them that he is slow to reveal himself.

"Children, have you any fish?" (John 21:5). Jesus asks in order to give. By his gentleness, he stirs up trust and generosity. Note also the way he likes to introduce himself by asking questions or making suggestions. Let us rejoice in the glory of Christ, Lord of the sea and of everything in it. Let us rejoice in this Lord of power who does not silence or crush, but befriends and consoles the human heart.

"Cast the net on the right side of the boat" (John 21:6). Just one word from Jesus obtains much more than we could ever hope for by our own strength. Talk to Jesus about how you have experienced (or not experienced) this reality in your own life. Ask him to make you more confident in his action and to increase your attentiveness to his words and the inspirations of his Holy Spirit.

Jesus is the mirror of the Father's providence. See how attentive he is to the disciples' hunger and fatigue. Like a good host, he prepares them a meal of roasted fish and bread. He asks that they contribute some of their catch and invites them to "come and eat." And all of them know that "it is the Lord."

Be present at the moment when Jesus looks upon Simon Peter and chooses him from among all the others: "Do you love me more than these?" *Do you love me?* This is the man to whom Jesus is going to entrust all his sheep and lambs. The apostolic mission to shepherd the flock is born of a loving surrender to Jesus. Now Peter's love is humble—tried by tribulation, not boasting of its human powers, knowing only how to trust itself to the knowledge and mercy of his Lord. "You know everything; you know that I love you" (John 21:17).

Rejoice in the lordship and majesty of Jesus, who generously offers Peter the chance to make up for his triple denial by this humble triple confession of his love. Try to penetrate the reaction of these two hearts—the Master and the disciple.

Let us be glad to see Christ's flock commended to the shepherd of his own choosing. Let us rejoice that Christ in his glory associates human beings to his work and gives them positions of such responsibility and honor.

For Reflection

Choose one or several of these Scripture passages to pray over. What connections can you find with the scene of Jesus preparing a lakeside breakfast for his hungry disciples?

- the feeding of the multitudes: Matthew 14:13-21; 15:32-38; Mark 6:32-44; Luke 9:10-17; John 6:1-13
- "I am the bread of life": John 6:22-71.

Contemplate the providence of God in the Church down through the ages.

The Church is Peter's boat, in which we face the sea. Spend some time thanking God for his glory revealed in this frail-looking vessel down through the centuries. So many sublime gestures of love and generosity, so many lives consecrated to God's service, so many sinners pardoned, so many varieties of sanctity. List a few of the things about the Church for which you are especially thankful to Jesus Christ.

Matthew 28:16-20; Mark 16:15-18

The Mission Transmitted

Words of St. Ignatius

Point One: At the command of the Lord the disciples go to Mount Tabor.

Point Two: Christ appears to them and says, "All power in heaven and on earth has been given to me."

Point Three: He sent them to preach throughout the whole world, saying: "Go, therefore, and teach all nations, baptizing them in the name of the Father and of the Son and of the Holy Spirit."

(Spiritual Exercises, 307)

Commentary

Jesus rebukes the disbelief and hardness of heart of the disciples who had failed to believe the eyewitness reports that Jesus was raised from the dead (Mark 16:14).

"Lord, will you at this time restore the kingdom to Israel?" (Acts 1:6). Right to the last hour, some disciples still cherish the hope that Jesus will act according to their human expectations. How slow-witted and dull we are in our aims, ambitions, and ways—until God's voice speaks and his hour sounds! Then, the Holy Spirit causes us to leave ourselves and changes us into authentic witnesses of Christ. No other power can work this change.

The aims of Jesus surpass all our human limitations and are not thwarted by our defects. "As the Father has sent me, even so I send you" (John 20:21). Conscious of his own sending by the Father, Jesus commissions others: "All authority in heaven and on earth has been given to me. Go therefore and make disciples . . . , baptizing . . . , teaching. . . . I will be with you" (Matthew 28:18-20).

Christ shares his powers with us for the ministry of salvation: "As each has received a gift, employ it for one another, as good stewards of God's varied grace . . . in order that in everything God may be glorified through Jesus Christ" (1 Peter 4:10-11).

". . . teaching them to observe all that I have commanded you" (Matthew 28:20). Christ's apostles do not draw out morality and dogma from their own ideas, nor do they compromise them through discussion or haggling. They are servants, not the Master. They have received a "deposit of faith" which must be conserved and transmitted intact (1 Timothy 6:20; 2 Timothy 1:14). This is their glory.

Let us rejoice over the glory and divine power of Christ, which reveals itself so splendidly in this universal mission on earth. How generously he has placed his powers into the fragile hands of human beings! How generous his promise of unerring assistance to the Church: "I will be with you always, to the close of the age" (Matthew 28:20).

Let us also be glad and rejoice at Christ's glory and joy in all those who will believe because of the apostles' preaching. What light and grace have spread out into the world through the Church's mission over the centuries!

For Reflection

St. Ignatius made this comment about evangelization: Even "among the angels no more noble exercises are found than the glorification of one's Creator and to bring back to Him his creatures, as far as they are able" (*Letter on Perfection*, n. 1).

What am I doing to respond to this call to incorporate others into Christ?
What are my chief obstacles?
Where do I most need Jesus' help?

Luke 24:50-53; Acts 1:1-14

The Ascension of Christ Our Lord

Words of St. Ignatius

Point One: After Christ our Lord had manifested himself for forty days to the Apostles, giving many proofs and signs and speaking about the Kingdom of God, he commanded them to wait in Jerusalem for the Holy Spirit who had been promised them.

Point Two: He led them out to Mount Olivet, and in their presence he was lifted up, and a cloud took him from their sight.

Point Three: While they are looking up to heaven the angels say to them, "Men of Galilee, why are you standing there looking up at the sky? This Jesus who has been taken up from you into heaven will return in the same way as you have seen him going into heaven."

(Spiritual Exercises, 312)

Commentary

We contemplate this mystery of the ascension in relation to our own exodus from ourselves and our self-centeredness. Jesus leads his flock beyond this limited and faulty perspective. It is good to see how much we need the Spirit to come and let us see life from the eternal point of view.

Luke's Gospel portrays Jesus going "up to Jerusalem" to accomplish our salvation. Jerusalem, the endpoint of this ascent, now becomes the point of departure towards the whole world. "You shall receive power when the Holy Spirit has come upon you; and you shall be my witnesses in Jerusalem and in all Judea and Samaria and to the end of the earth" (Acts 1:8). The Holy Spirit is the gift of gifts, "the promise of my Father" (Luke 24:49). The Spirit, when he comes, will teach the disciples everything, showing them how to preach conversion and the forgiveness of sins (24:46-48). They need not fear. The Spirit will give them words to confound their persecutors and accusers.

After Jesus ascended into heaven, the disciples did not remain sad, as at the Last Supper. Instead, "they returned to Jerusalem with great joy" (Luke 24: 52). Then they gathered in the upper room and "devoted themselves to prayer" (Acts 1:14). With Mary, the Mother of the Church, they persevered in prayer, united in spirit as they awaited the Spirit. The celestial life begins to flower. The ascension: Jesus in the heavens. Where our treasure is, there will our hearts be. Seek the things that are above; taste the things that are above (Matthew 6:21,33).

The cloud that took Jesus out of the disciples' sight speaks of the fact that all earthly experience will be transcended. Every part of our being will be spiritualized! The soul's union with God drives out all natural malevolence and every trace of self-love. In this way, the entire human person, body and soul, becomes a docile instrument of the Spirit. Christ's definitive triumph has accomplished this!

For Reflection

If someone were to ask me why Christ's ascension is cause for rejoicing, what would I say?

____

____

____

____

____

Mary and the disciples devoted themselves to prayer as they awaited the gift of the Holy Spirit. Do I pray for this gift as well? How can I become more aware of the Spirit and my need for him?

Contemplation to Attain Love

This contemplation is the crowning moment of the *Exercises*. Also, as St. Ignatius recommended to his followers, it suggests a method of praying which is perfect for use in ordinary life by those who have fully lived the experience of the *Spiritual Exercises*.

St. Ignatius offers two preliminary observations to keep in mind throughout this contemplation:

- *Love ought to manifest itself more by deeds than by words.*
- *Love consists in a mutual communication between the two persons. That is, the one who loves gives and communicates to the beloved what he or she has or can have; and the beloved in return does the same to the lover. Thus, if the one has knowledge, one gives it to the other who does not; and similarly in regard to honors or riches. Each shares with the other.*

(Spiritual Exercises, 230-232)

Words of St. Ignatius

After the usual *preparatory prayer, I see myself as standing before God our Lord, and also before the angels and saints, who are interceding for me. . . .*

I ask for what I desire. Here it will be to ask for interior knowledge of all the great good I have received, in order that, stirred to profound gratitude, I may become able to love and serve the Divine Majesty in all things.

I consider four points:

Point One: I will call back into my memory the gifts I have received—my creation, redemption, and other gifts particularly to myself. I will ponder with deep affection how much God our Lord has done for me, and how much he has given me of what he possesses, and consequently how he, the same Lord, desires to give me even his very self, in accordance with his divine design.

Then I will reflect on myself, and consider what I on my part ought in all reason and justice to offer and give to the Divine Majesty, namely, all my possessions, and myself along with them. I will speak as one making an offering with deep affection, and say:

"Take, Lord, and receive all my liberty, my memory, my understanding, and all my will—all that I have and possess. You, Lord, have given all that to me. I now give it back to you, O Lord. All of

it is yours. Dispose of it according to your will. Give me love of yourself along with your grace, for that is enough for me."

Point Two: I will consider how God dwells in creatures; in the elements, giving them existence; in the plants, giving them life; in the animals, giving them sensation; in human beings, giving them intelligence; and finally, how in this way he dwells also in myself, giving me existence, life, sensation, and intelligence; and even further, making me his temple, since I am created as a likeness and image of the Divine Majesty. Then once again I will reflect on myself, in the manner described in the first point, or in any other way I feel to be better. This same procedure will be used in each of the following points.

Point Three: I will consider how God labors and works for me in all the creatures on the face of the earth; that is, he acts in the manner of one who is laboring. For example, he is working in the heavens, elements, plants, fruits, cattle, and all the rest—giving them their existence, conserving them, concurring with their vegetative and sensitive activities, and so forth. Then I will reflect on myself.

Point Four: I will consider how all good things and gifts descend from above; for example, my limited power from the Supreme and Infinite Power above; and so of justice, goodness, piety, mercy, and so forth — as the rays come down from the sun, or the rains from their source. Then I will finish by reflecting on myself, as has been explained. I will conclude with a colloquy and an Our Father.

(Spiritual Exercises, 232-237)

For Reflection

The grace requested in this contemplation is to recognize how much you owe to God's love and to make the wholehearted response of your love that will express your gratitude. As you seek this grace, be conscious that intercessors are present with you. Which angels, saints, or other holy men and women have you turned to in the past? Take a minute to identify them, and picture them praying for you now.

Commentary

By the time you arrive at this high point, the summit of the *Exercises*, you have already embraced God's will over your life. Having made every effort to strip yourself of disordered inclinations, you are trying to identify completely with Christ and to focus on serving and praising his divine Majesty. More and more, you desire only to respond to the impulses of God's love, which "has been poured into our hearts through the Holy Spirit which is given to us" (Romans 5:5). This love is not a matter of mere sentiment or words, says St. Ignatius. It expresses itself "in deed and in truth" (1 John 3:18). In this way, love becomes a donation of oneself, a mutual exchange with the beloved of all what we are and that we possess.

Here, St. Ignatius says that the way to attain love is to become able—under the power of the Spirit—to see yourself and your entire life history as a continuous loving gift from God. This means pondering the gift of creation; you meditate on having been brought into existence into a universe that was also created by God, on being continually sustained by God's loving care.

Joyfully sifting through each of the details that make up this overall gift is the work of contemplation. There are so many concrete expressions of divine love to consider: my eyes, the light, the landscape before me, my heart, my intelligence, my ability to express myself, the air that I breathe, beauty, love, life. . . . There are the countless blessings devolving from Christ's incarnation and redemption. . . . And how long the chain of particular graces through which this redemption has touched my own life: through my family, my education, my calling, the Church, baptism, preaching, good examples, inner movements of grace.

I must ponder and contemplate how God has given himself to me in so many ways. He has made himself my traveling companion, coming to me as brother and friend—even giving himself as food and going so far as to make me a partaker in his own divine nature (2 Peter 1:4).

Let your feelings of love and gratitude well up into a prayer of self-offering to God, as St. Ignatius suggests: *Take, Lord, and receive, all my liberty, my memory, my understanding, and all my will . . .* (*Spiritual Exercises*, 234).

For Reflection

Make a list of some of the gifts of God for which you are especially grateful. You might even consider praying through it as a sort of litany, in the style of Psalm 136, with the refrain: "Give thanks to the Lord, for he is good."

It is one and the same Lord who shows his love in diverse ways, drawing us through so many gifts. As St. Ignatius once wrote, "the divine majesty is to be found in all things through his presence, power, and essence."

Consider the loving presence of God dwelling in all things. He gives existence to everything—giving growth to plants, sensation and movement to animals, intelligence and love to spiritual beings. He is within me with all these forms of his presence and with another marvelous gift besides: the grace which makes me his living temple.

Discovering this loving presence of God leaves the soul wounded by love. This is a great grace, to be ardently sought and desired. "Reveal Your presence," St. John of the Cross used to say, "and may the vision of Your beauty be my death; for the sickness of love is not cured except by Your very presence and image" (*Spiritual Canticle*, v. 11). Love that is activated in response to God's love will move the soul to become present to its loving Lord in all things, recognizing and loving him in them.

For Reflection

What do these Scripture passages contribute to your understanding of what it means to be God's temple?

"Jesus answered him, 'Those who love me will keep my word, and my Father will love them, and we will come to them and make our home with them'" (John 14:23).

"For we are the temple of the living God; as God said, 'I will live in them and move among them, and I will be their God, and they shall be my people'" (2 Corinthians 6:16).

"Do you not know that you are God's temple and that God's Spirit dwells in you? If any one destroys God's temple, God will destroy him. For God's temple is holy, and that temple you are" (1 Corinthians 3:16-17).

"Do you not know that your body is a temple of the Holy Spirit within you, which you have from God? You are not your own; you were bought with a price. So glorify God in your body" (1 Corinthians 6:19-20).

In Everything, God Acts for My Good. God inspires my love through his loving action in all the things and events around me. His love is always active on behalf of human beings—not only because divine cooperation is necessary for the functioning of the universe, but also because he watches over all of us directly, through his providence. No hair of my head falls without the Father's knowing it. And if not even one lowly sparrow is forgotten by God, I can proceed unafraid, knowing myself to be "of more value than many sparrows" (Luke 12:7).

"We know that in everything God works for good with those who love him" (Romans 8:28). Everything testifies to this: the birds of the air, the flowers of the field, the grain of wheat, the work of the miller, the consecration of the priest, the sacraments, and the wonders which will accompany the work of God's messengers (Mark 16:20).

As I discover this loving, constant action of God in all things, my soul will feel the desire to respond with an active love—to direct all my plans, actions, and accomplishments towards God's service and praise and to convert all my life into a continuous act of love. I will discover how to make my every word or deed an act of thanksgiving and an opportunity for loving service.

God Is the Very Good Who Calls Forth My Love. It is God himself who lays claim to the love of the soul. Everything that attracts me in his creatures—any power, justice, goodness, beauty, piety, mercy, or other quality—is only a reflection of their Creator's infinite perfections and attractions. They merely participate in the highest and infinite power, justice, and goodness of God. As rays of light descend from the sun and streams flow down from the fountain, every good and precious gift descends from above (James 1:17).

As I come to see God as the source of everything that is good, I will consider it an obligation of love to keep before me this connection between the Giver and his gifts. I will desire to give to God all the glory and credit for his gifts and qualities—even those that other people may say they find in me! I will faithfully give God loving and grateful praise for every good, power, wisdom, and beauty that I contemplate in any creature. I will love God in all things, and all things in him.

For Reflection

End with some resolutions and reflections centered on the three basic questions you considered in the very first exercise:

- What has Christ desired to love through me?
- What does Christ desire to do through me?
- What shall I do to love and serve Christ?

"I am the vine, you are the branches," Jesus said (John 15:5). The image describes relationships within Christ's body, the Church. Just as no branch can live if the sap ceases to flow through it, no part of this body can function or even exist apart from its Head. Being rightly connected is a question of life and death. This is why, at the end of the *Exercises*, St. Ignatius offers some "rules," or guidelines, to orient us in our daily lives as members of the Church.

Commentary

In our day, as in his, many people have misguided ideas about the Church. Some imagine it as a utopia for saints only. Others consider it something purely interior and private, with no other norms than their own personal inspiration. In search of a "purer gospel" or a "more mature" Christian liberty, they have lost what St. Ignatius called *the genuine attitude which we ought to maintain in the Church* (*Spiritual Exercises*, 352).

The remedy for this situation is for each member of the Church to come in living contact with the Christ of the gospels. This is what the *Exercises* have encouraged you to do. If there is any key for interpreting them, it lies in St. Paul's exhortations to follow Christ in his humility and self-emptying (Philippians 2:7-8), his way of authentic freedom (Galatians 5:1), and his obedience (Romans 5:19).

To the extent that the *Exercises* achieve their goal in you, you will find that the figure of the Church shines more and more brightly. More clearly and insistently than before, you will grasp that Christ, the historical figure who lived in Palestine and now reigns in glory in heaven, intended to continue his saving and sanctifying action in the world by means of the Church.

With this discovery, all of the reverent, enlightened, and generous love with which you have become bound to Christ will also transfer to the body that continues his life on earth. The Church is the context for love's practical application, the living milieu in which we receive the life of Christ. Here we live and grow according to his plans for the glory of the Father.

To accept the divine plans for our salvation and sanctification in the Church is to embrace the will of God, which draws us by the means *he* chooses and not by our own preferences. We may feel tempted, at times, to pursue an illusory "maturity" by declaring our independence from God's designs and going our own way, with our own resources. For St. Ignatius, however, this is never an option. The Ignatian way is one of loving attachment toward everything that reveals God's will. It means overflowing with joy and thanksgiving by putting your own will at the service of God's and feeling guided by him—though along paths you do not always comprehend. St. Ignatius yearned to submit himself to God, not to his own whims or desires for "self-fulfillment," when he wrote these norms for living in the Church. As the Second Vatican Council affirmed, this attitude is what it means to live in the faith of the Church:

> This sacred Synod teaches that by divine institution bishops have succeeded to the place of the apostles as shepherds of the Church, and that he who hears them, hears Christ, while he who rejects them, rejects Christ and Him who sent Christ (Luke 10:16). (*Lumen Gentium*, 20)

> This is the unique Church of Christ. . . . After His Resurrection our Savior handed her over to Peter to be shepherded (John 21:17), commissioning him and the other apostles to propagate and govern her (Matthew 28:18ff). He erected her for all ages as "the pillar and mainstay of the truth" (1 Timothy 3:15).(*Lumen Gentium*,8)

Ready to Obey the Will of God. St. Ignatius' "rules" or guidelines for viewing the Church arise from the context of joyous faith, and they call for actions that arise from it as well. The first rule summarizes this faith in strong and spare language: *With all judgment of our own put aside, we ought to keep our minds disposed and ready to be obedient in everything to the true Spouse of Christ our Lord, which is our holy Mother the hierarchical Church* (*Spiritual Exercises*, 353).

This does not mean abdicating our responsibility to use our minds. It does mean being willing to recognize that, for many reasons, our personal judgments and viewpoints are often in error. St. Ignatius indicates that this is certainly the case when we insist that something is white, while the Church—speaking with the authority it has received from God—has declared that it is black. We have to humbly admit that even in human affairs we are prone to error. How much more so in matters that surpass our natural capacities—matters related to revealed truths or to the inscrutable ways by which God draws us to himself!

Trusting in God means trusting that he will guide us through the means he has provided. As St. Ignatius' thirteenth guideline puts it: *For it is by the same Spirit and Lord of ours who gave the ten commandments that our Holy Mother Church is guided and governed* (*Spiritual Exercises*, 365; see also Matthew 19:16-19 and *Lumen Gentium* 4,7).

If we live and act out of this loving perspective of faith, we stand convinced that everything the Church authoritatively approves and encourages for the good of souls is good and should be praised and encouraged. This is the guiding insight that underlies the practical orientations that St. Ignatius' presents in eight "rules" concerning things that "we should praise." Among those St. Ignatius mentions are confession to a priest, frequent reception of the Eucharist, the Mass, hymns, prayers, religious services, the religious life, virginity, relics, indulgences, fasting, and the precepts of the Church (*Spiritual Exercises*, 354-361).

Ignatius did not naïvely assume that it was impossible for human beings to introduce defects into practices like these. In fact, he had considerable experience of human imperfections and strove to correct them. However, he recognized the practices as good in themselves and saw that the way to purify them is to practice them well, in spirit and in truth. St. Ignatius offered this positive resolution to live in the faith of the Church: to praise what the Church praises, and to praise more what the Church praises more.

The same attitude of discreet charity is also called for when it becomes necessary to help correct the defects in conduct of people who have been placed in highly visible positions of authority. To do this while avoiding all scandal takes delicacy and personal sacrifice, but this is what sincerity requires when it is informed by charity and is not merely an outlet for pride, vengeance, or impatience. If the people who have the faults are able to remedy them, we may be in a position to speak to them directly. Otherwise, it may be our responsibility to follow the proper channels and seek out the persons who can provide a remedy (*Spiritual Exercises*, 362).

Avoiding Factions. St. Ignatius was very concerned about the consequences of divisiveness in the Church—factions, loss of respect for the truth, doctrinal deviations, and even heresy and scandal. His "rules" therefore contain various warnings about how to avoid it. To preserve unity, Ignatius refused to take sides in a running debate that pitted scholastic theology against positive theology. Instead, he praised both for their specific contributions and pointed out their complementarity (*Spiritual Exercises*, 363).

In other matters, too, St. Ignatius urged a unifying balance. Faith and works must not be separated, for example; faith, informed by charity, translates into good works. Similarly, we must never speak of grace in a way excludes freedom, nor of freedom in a way that obscures the need for grace (*Spiritual Exercises*, 368-369). Certainly, some of these controversies are still with us. If he were alive today, though, St. Ignatius might frame his solution to divisiveness using other examples.

We can think of many other situations where the Ignatian "rule" for avoiding contention would be useful. For example, we must not dismiss the law and its obligations when we exercise personal discernment; however, the law must be applied in a way that recognizes its own distinctions about matters of greater or lesser importance, along with the need to apply moral judgment to particular individual cases. We cannot exalt the charisms and forget about submitting these possible gifts to the discernment of the authority for the common good (see *Lumen*

Gentium, 12); on the other hand, authority must not neglect its duty of promoting true charisms.

It's Attitude that Counts. As you can see, the *attitudes* that St. Ignatius recommends are more important than the concrete examples provided to explain them. Problems change over time. Some become more acute, some fade away, new ones spring up. Through it all, the important thing is to joyfully and gratefully live out the faith of the Church, in the Church, and to accept the stands that this faith requires—with reverence, love, and discretion.

St. Ignatius especially urges confidence in Christ, who helps his Church and guides it through the Spirit, today as always. As this confidence grows, you develop a response of *reverent and loving attention, of joy and thankfulness to the Lord*, who has allowed you to live in the Church, under the guidance of our pastors in communion with the Supreme Pastor of the flock, his Vicar on earth.

The faith and love which we owe to Christ will be manifest in our humble, concrete, and joyful fidelity to the Church. We will be conscious that we are working for Christ, and he in us, in his design of universal salvation. You have a part in this plan—a part that God has specially chosen and designed for you and that will continue to unfold. Embrace it, as he has shown you through these *Spiritual Exercises*, and know the joy of living for the greater glory of God!

For Reflection

When Jesus was on earth, he related to the Father with humble obedience. What does his example show me about the way I should relate to the Church? Is there anything I need to repent of and change in my attitude and my actions?

___

___

___

___

___

___

___

___

___

Do I contribute to the divisiveness within the Church? How might I apply St. Ignatius' approach to avoiding factions? How can I pursue the things that make for peace?

Reflect on Christ's promise to guide the Church and on the part he invites you to play in his plan of salvation. Express your thoughts—your faith, thanks, joy, and even your questions—to him in a prayer.

About the Author and the Translator

Manuel Ruiz Jurado, S.J., is a Jesuit priest of the Province of Spain. Born in Andalucia, Fr. Ruiz is President Emeritus of the Institute of Spirituality of the Pontifical Gregorian University in Rome. Fr. Ruiz is a specialist in Ignatian Spirituality and the history of the Jesuits, and an author of numerous studies and review articles on the life and spirituality of St. Ignatius of Loyola and the Society of Jesus. He has produced several critical editions of the writings of the first Jesuits and written various historical works and theological studies. Each summer, Fr. Ruiz offers the full course of the *Spiritual Exercises* to the students of the Gregorian University, as well as shorter courses and days of recollection throughout the year. This is Fr. Ruiz's first work to appear in English.

Robert Hurd, S.J., is a native of San Francisco, California, and a Jesuit priest of the California Province of the Society of Jesus. He began his translation of this book while a doctoral student at the Pontifical Gregorian University in Rome from 1993-1997. Fr. Hurd has been a pastoral minister at Our Lady of Guadalupe Church and a physician at La Clínica Tepeyac in Denver, Colorado.

A RADICAL LOVE
Wisdom from
Dorothy Day
WELCOMING THE NEW MILLENNIUM
MY HEART SPEAKS
Wisdom from
Pope John XXIII
LIVE JESUS!
LOVE SONGS
Wisdom from
WALKING WITH THE FATHER
TOUCHING THE RISEN CHRIST
Wisdom from
The Fathers
HOLD FAST TO GOD
EVEN UNTO DEATH
Wisdom from
Modern Martyrs